# EXCLUSIVE PEDIGREE

## My life in and out of the Brethren

### By John L. Fear

Edited by

Robert Fear

Dedicated to

Alexander, Joseph and Jessica

# TABLE OF CONTENTS

# INTRODUCTION

Like many eldest sons, I rebelled against my father during my teenage years. Fortunately, unlike many, I had a chance of reconciliation before he passed away and this book is the end result.

My father, John, was born into a religious sect known as the Exclusive Brethren. This sheltered him from the outside world as he grew up but could not hide him from its influences. A struggle began in his mind that eventually led to him leaving the Brethren, along with his young family.

This is a story that John wanted told. Over the last couple of years of his life he spent many hours writing up his memoirs with the aim of completing a book about his life and experiences. During his last few months John grew weaker and was physically unable to complete this task. It was around this time that my mother approached me to see if I could help. I was more than happy to assist and started typing up his notes on my computer.

Reconciliation was difficult as neither of us really understood each other's point of view. Working on my father's life story taught me a lot about what he had been through and helped me appreciate the sacrifices both my parents had made. In return I got a sense of understanding from John about the way I approached the world.

After his death a limited edition of Exclusive Pedigree was printed in paperback format for members of the family, especially Alexander, Joseph and Jessica, his young grandchildren, so they would know who he is and was. John wrote most of the book himself but it was still incomplete when he died. A lot of the remaining chapters were compiled from his diary notes and letters that he wrote home. The final chapters were written by my younger brother, Alastair.

It was only recently, while visiting Mary, my wonderful mother, that a chance remark spurred me into action. She mentioned that it had always been John's ambition to have his memoirs published properly.

My intention, by publishing this book, is to belatedly make my father's dream come true.


Robert Fear, Eastbourne, June 2016

# PROLOGUE

The pages that follow are in response to those friends who have said to me, "You must have had an interesting life; you ought to write about it". I have always found a first person story absorbing and as my life seems to fall naturally into eight phases, I have divided these memoirs into eight chronological parts. It will be well worth the effort if these pages are read by my grandchildren, so they will know who their Grandpa John is and was. I have a theory that the more you know about a person the more you will understand and make allowances for their mistakes and I hope that family and friends will feel able to do that. Having said this, I feel some misgivings that the spotlight will fall too much on me but I write with the constant desire, "To God be the glory".

My memory of early events and the emotions that accompanied them have diminished with the passage of time. I also have the disadvantage of not having kept a regular diary so I simply write about those incidents and identify the turning points that I can clearly remember. To keep the narrative flowing I have avoided, with a few exceptions, any knowledge of events as they later developed. I have also occasionally digressed from a strict chronological sequence to write, in detail, about certain subjects that have had a formative influence on my life. I hope these chapters will be of general interest but this arrangement gives the reader the option of dipping into or skipping over these subjects according to their personal interests.

As my own mother and father and my wife's parents are no longer with us, I am able to be more candid than I would have been otherwise. However, out of respect for the feelings of other relatives and friends, it is not as full a disclosure as it might be but it is, at least, the story that can be told.

When I first discussed the writing of this autobiography with a possible publisher, I was told that it would be a best-selling book if I felt able to 'blow the whistle' on Billy Graham and expose the inner workings of the Exclusive Brethren cult. I made it clear that during my years of association with Billy Graham, I had never known him to behave in any way that would be incompatible with his high calling as a Christian evangelist. I also told the publisher that I had left behind many God fearing relatives and friends in the Exclusive Brethren system and would not write anything that could cause them distress. I make this point clear at the beginning of the book so that no-one acquires a copy under the false impression that it will 'blow the top' on these two important aspects of my life.

Although I am only a few years short of the Psalmist's span of three score years and ten, my life seems to have been an incredibly short one and the passing of the years have speeded up with the passage of time. Having had a couple of near encounters with the 'last enemy', I am now so grateful for the bonus of each new day. I am more convinced than ever, despite arguments to the contrary that, "God is inconceivably nicer than we've ever given Him credit for".


John L Fear, Cumnor, Oxford, August 1993

# PART 1 - CHILDHOOD YEARS

Father as a young man

Mother as a young woman

# Chapter 1 - Infant Memories

Unusually perhaps, I have four specific memories of things that happened between my first and second birthdays. These memories are as vivid now as when I first experienced them.

The first infant memory is associated with my much loved mother. We were on holiday at the time, in grandma's home, situated in the South Wales mining village of Basaleg. This was the home to some five hundred men who worked in the local coal mines, slate quarries and steel mills. Villagers could not hang out washing on the line or leave babies outside in prams because of the pervading black dust from the mines' molten slag heaps and the red dust from the steel works. The village came to life each morning shortly before sunrise as the 'knocker-up' man tapped his long steel-tipped pole on the bedroom windows of those workers who had registered for his services.

During the next few minutes the whole village echoed to the sound of hob-nailed boots, as the miners, wearing flat caps and mufflers, clattered noisily across the bridge leading to the pits. Ten hours later, the weary colliers trudged back, with blackened faces, after their long, harsh day of labour deep in the bowels of the earth.

Meanwhile, I eagerly looked forward to the time each day when my mother lifted me up so that I could sit on top of the wall of the bridge. At most times the bridge was deserted but occasionally a group of retired or sick miners gathered there to exchange village gossip, reminisce on the good old days and puff reflectively on their battered clay pipes. After a while I became aware that the sharp coping tiles were cutting into my bare legs but nothing could detract from the sheer delight of watching the crystal clear waters of the stream as they rushed, glistened and heaved over a series of tiny falls.

The bridge which was skilfully built by earlier stone masons has now sadly disappeared. During a recent visit to Basaleg I found that the bridge, together with the lines of slate covered miners' cottages, had been bulldozed. The mines, which provided work for the colliers and supported a vibrant community, were closed down in favour of cheap imported coal, offshore oil and a network of risky nuclear power stations. The vast concrete viaduct that now straddles the remains of Basaleg is lit, night and day, by glaring orange tungsten lamps that illuminate the headlong rush of heavy lorries, buses and cars from the Severn Bridge to the coastal resorts of South Wales. The stream's fate is equally tragic. Its waters now flow for miles underground through an ugly concrete pipe to join up with other anonymous streams that feed the waters of the Bristol Channel. The process is known in the construction industry by that equally ugly word, culverted.

My other infant memories can be described more briefly. It may not have been, and probably was not, the first time that I had wet my cot. However, I vividly recall one particular night when I woke up to a pleasant warm feeling which in time gave way to a wet patch that gradually grew and became unhappily cold. Worse followed when my grumpy father covered the lumpy, damp mattress with a smelly rubber sheet and left me to ponder how this disaster could have happened. I can, even now, recall the hot tears of shame that scalded my face as sleep eluded me throughout the remainder of that long night.

I also number among my earliest memories the not unpleasant smell of herbs which my father regularly brewed, in a galvanised zinc bath, on top of the old gas stove in the kitchen. These herbs provided basic ingredients for the tinctures and ointments dispensed for patients who consulted him as a medical herbalist.

The remaining memory was when I reached the age of eighteen months, mother arrived home after several days of unexplained absence. She carried in her arms a vociferous bundle that turned out to hold my baby brother, Paul, who suddenly became a rival claimant to my mother's affection. I remember that he smelled of milk. After a short time Paul spent the night in my room. He slept in a cot next to my bed and cried on and off during the whole night.

These then were the sights, sounds and smells that evoked my earliest memories. I often wonder why I can recall these insignificant events in such vivid detail, but I am grateful for the security and love I felt during my infancy.

# Chapter 2 - Exclusive Background

I have been unable to discover how my parents came to meet each other. They certainly had quite different family backgrounds. Mother and her two siblings were brought up by their widowed mother, Annie Eleanor Coslett (later Harwood), in a small miner's cottage in the industrial Welsh village of Basaleg. The view from grandma's front window was dominated by a huge slag heap which was an accumulation of waste excavated, over the years, from the village coal mine.

Compared with the straightened circumstances of my mother's family, my father was brought up in a relatively affluent home. His family lived in a three storey town house in the residential area of Bedminster in Bristol. This was within walking distance of the Clifton Downs and the famous Suspension Bridge that spanned the Avon.

In view of their different social backgrounds and the distance that separated their homes, there is little doubt that the one thing they had in common brought them together. This was the fact that Paul and Bertha's families both belonged to the small and secretive Christian sect, now known as the Exclusive Brethren. It is purely speculative but I think it quite likely that they met in Newport at one of the regular monthly fellowship gatherings that were held in the area covering Bristol and South Wales. The Exclusives only permitted their young people to marry someone from their own restricted circle and so these Saturday meetings, held ostensibly for ministry, served to introduce single youngsters to potential life partners who lived within easy travelling distance of their respective homes. My parents were 23 when they married in 1925 but remained deeply in love until they both died, within a few days of each other, in October 1991. To the very end of their lives both parents remained implacably loyal to the extreme and increasingly manipulative leadership and teachings of the Exclusive Brethren. For this reason four of their six children were sadly denied any contact with them during the last twenty five years of their lives.

The original Brethren movement (often referred to as the Plymouth Brethren) began in Dublin in 1825. It claimed to be a reaction against the spiritual deadness of the established churches of the day. The early Brethren leaders stated that their desire was to restore the simplicity of worship and gospel witness that characterised the life of the early Church. They also expressed their intention to be free of all authority or traditions outside the letter of Scripture. They recognised no ministerial order in the administration of the Sacraments of the Church, Baptism and Holy Communion. One of the founding leaders, John Nelson Darby, outlined his objection to the exercise of any clerical office in the Church in a book, curiously entitled, *The notion of a clergyman - dispensationally the sin against the Holy Spirit*. The Brethren fervently believed in the imminence of Christ's second coming and in consequence they had a strong interest in the study of Biblical prophecy. Our Lord's second advent was frequently referred to in the weekly Gospel sermon, preferably and hopefully in the preacher's own lifetime. We were warned that the Lord would come back when we least expected Him ("... like a thief in the night") and only those who deserved it would, "rise to meet Him in the air".

When I was six or seven, my parents led me to believe that I was quite a naughty boy and I constantly lived with the expectation that I would be left behind when Jesus came back to take the 'elect' to Heaven. On one occasion, when I came home from school, mother was not where I had grown accustomed to finding her. No one will ever know the fear that paralysed me as I immediately concluded that the Lord had indeed returned, taken my parents and left me behind. I was immeasurably relieved when she eventually walked into the room.

In 1845 the Exclusive minority broke away from the mainstream of the movement (widely known as the Open Brethren). From that time a system of centralised control began to govern the administration of all their Assemblies, the name that identified the Exclusives' local churches. Such local autonomy, as there was, ceased to exist and the increasing emphasis on 'separation from the world' introduced elements of legalism which the leaders of the Brethren had earlier renounced. The Exclusives abandoned the original principle of mixing freely with other believers and this separatist stance led them to bar Christians, not in their fellowship, from participation in the Communion Service. In due course they gave up the missionary enterprises that motivated the Brethren from the start of the movement. Darby, who led the breakaway, had an acrimonious relationship with former friends who remained with the Open Brethren and this breach has not been healed to this day.

I will explain later on how the strict regime of the Exclusive Brethren had a profound effect on every sphere of our lives. As their views on relationships, finance, education and employment were taught by persuasive leaders, it was difficult not to conform to their rules. In the 1950's and 60's Exclusive leaders applied even more extreme regulations to the lives of their members and it was a very traumatic period in my life.

# Chapter 3 - Early Childhood

My childhood took place in interesting times. It spanned the decade and a half (1929-1945) that was probably the most eventful period of the 20th Century. Those who escaped the economic devastation that was caused by the Stock Market Crash of 1929 were faced with mass unemployment during the depression years of the 1930's and the appalling slaughter that blighted the western world during the Second World War. I was three when Hitler came to power in Germany and fifteen when the war ended in 1945 but I cannot recall being unduly disturbed by all the momentous events of those first turbulent years of my life. This was due in no small part to the protective and loving environment provided by my parents and our local Brethren Assembly.

My parents' first home was in the Leicestershire village of Kirby Muxloe. This still exists as a rural hamlet on the northern outskirts of the city of Leicester. It has its own church, shop, pub and substantial remains of the village's only notable feature - Kirby Muxloe Castle. We lived in one of a row of tiny, derelict looking thatched cottages and our home is named on my Birth Certificate as 'Eben-ezer'. I remember little of it, except that it depended for its lighting on a couple of incandescent gas mantles and for its heating on a temperamental cast iron coke stove. It had a dank little back garden that was crawling with woodlice, snails, cockroaches and beetles. The walls were covered with lichen and moss. In autumn a cold, damp, earthy odour pervaded the atmosphere around the cottages.

Our next family home was an equally undistinguished terraced house in a Coronation Street style road on a rather dreary council estate in one of Leicester's suburbs, known as Clarendon Park. The combined weekly rent and rates, in today's money, was 20 pence.

Within eight years of my parents' marriage, in 1925, they were blessed with the arrival of four children. I was born in October 1929 - the year when Bleriot flew across the English Channel and as one commentator said, "England ceased to be an island". Paul was born when I was eighteen months old and he was soon followed by Ruth Elizabeth Anne and David. My mother then gave birth to twins but they failed to survive a difficult childbirth. Robert James Rufus and Florence Mary completed the family a few years later.

The kitchen door of our new home in Leicester opened on to a back yard. It had a tiny oblong of lawn that led to two adjoining brick outhouses. These were built back to back with our neighbours' identical outhouses. One was used for the storage of coal, chopped firewood and paraffin. A multi-purpose galvanised zinc bath hung from a nail on the back of the door. This bath was used by my father for brewing up his herbal remedies, by my mother for her twice weekly family wash and by all of us for our Saturday evening bath night. Once in a while the same zinc bath was used for the baptism of the latest Fear baby, in a sacrament known by the Brethren as Household Baptism. The second outhouse was called the privy, as it accommodated our one and only lavatory. It was considered to be modern because it had a built-in water cistern rather than the more common means of sewage disposal for a Victorian house of that age, an earth or chemical closet. Some of our neighbours, who lived in posher houses on the estate, had two and three holed privies and an outside wash-house. Our privy had two heart-shaped holes cut out of the door.

A yew tree grew alongside the privy wall, presumably for its sanitary effect. Father warned us against eating any of the tree which he said was poisonous. Six foot high brick walls separated our back yard from three of our adjoining neighbours. The only other plants that tolerated such impoverished growing conditions were a clump of rhubarb, a straggly lilac bush and some tufts of horseradish, from which my father made sauce. When I was about twelve, I had the never-to-be-forgotten task of peeling and grating the horseradish root in preparation for the sauce. Grating the root releases a powerful, volatile oil which rushes up the nostrils and clears out any traces of blocked sinuses. Horseradish loses its pungency when cooked, so the sauce is made by adding vinegar and cream to the raw grated roots.

Owing to the restricted and sunless space in our back yard we played either in the street or, when one of our parents would take us, in the nearby park. For our street games we shared a battered old tricycle, a handful of marbles and a football. We also played conkers. This is a game still played by boys wherever horse chestnut trees are to be found. A hole is bored through each horse chestnut and a piece of string threaded through the hole. Boys strike their opponents' conker until one of them breaks. The winner is the boy whose chestnut remains intact. It was called a 'oncer' and each subsequent win was added to the conker's score. Serious competitors bake their conkers or soak them in vinegar to make them tougher. When we were on our own we played solitary games such as 'whip and top' or bowling a ball underarm at a set of stumps chalked on the back wall of our entry passage. In the park we wrestled with a score of other children for turns on the few swings that still worked. All of the playground equipment was red with rust and most of it squeaked noisily owing to years of neglect by the elderly park-keeper.

Occasionally we were treated to a Saturday afternoon visit to Leicester Museum. It was only a ten minute walk across the park. The museum is still a few hundred yards down a rural lane, known as New Walk, which has since become famous as the first example of pedestrianisation in Britain. The museum's entrance hall was dominated by a stuffed and badly moth eaten twenty foot high giraffe. In the galleries, which surrounded the giraffe's head, we gazed at glass cases that exhibited scores of assorted stuffed birds and mammals. However, the exhibit that invariably drew me, like a magnet, was the Egyptian mummy which had toes sticking out from its partially bandaged feet.

During the long summer holidays we spent one special day visiting a dairy farm about three miles from our home. We enjoyed every minute of our walk into the countryside. Long before we got to the farm we began to pick up the pungent smell of cows and their manure. The farmer's wife was at the gate to welcome us. We drank warm, fresh milk from a big churn. Pint and half pint measures were hanging inside the milk churn. In addition to the milk, mother bought a half pound pat of soft yellow butter and a couple of duck eggs. On the way back home, along Shady Lane, we sat down in a meadow for a picnic tea. Mother divided a fresh loaf of bread into chunks on which she generously spread our newly acquired butter. Before we left the meadow we picked enough wild flowers to make several daisy, buttercup and clover chains. It was a sublime, carefree day under blue skies.

Some summer holidays were spent on the East Anglian coast in resorts such as Heacham and Skegness. Our parents used to hire a beach hut, which was our base for the day. We had a fully cooked meal at lunch-time - this was grilled on a pump-up methylated spirits primus stove. We spent the rest of the day chasing around sand dunes, paddling in the shallow sea, building sandcastles, collecting seaweed and shells. In our childhood days we could reach the East Coast resorts in about two hours by mainline steam train. On the way we broke our journey at Kings Lynn where we brought a good stock of food and other items for our holiday. If we went by car we also had day trips to Cromer but Great Yarmouth was off limits because it had a row of amusement arcades.

# Chapter 4 - Primary School

I began to attend primary school at the age of five. The nearest one to our home was St. John the Baptist School. This was a Church of England school and it was here that I realised, for the first time, that conflicts would arise between those of us brought up in a strict Exclusive Brethren home and the world outside. It was quite a painful awakening and even at that young age I remember blaming my parents for neglecting to prepare me for these difficulties.

The problem arose immediately when I returned home after my first day at school. I told my parents that school began with a religious meeting. They appeared to know nothing about the daily act of worship known as Morning Assembly. They asked questions about it and my father grew increasingly stern-faced as I told him about the hymns, Bible reading and the religious talk by the Vicar. Father told me I would not be allowed to attend Morning Assembly in future and to enforce his wishes he marched me off to school on the following morning.

I sat all alone, underneath rows of partially filled coat pegs, for what seemed like an eternity. The sound of hymn singing drifted from the nearby hall and I wished with all my heart that I could have been with the other children. Eventually my father reappeared in the company of the Headmaster. They had apparently agreed that I would be exempted from attending Morning Assembly and all other religious activities in future. This seemed to create a precedent because, at first, I was left alone in an empty classroom during the thirty minute assemblies. There must have been further discussion on the subject because, after a while, a teacher would sit with me. Once a month, the entire school attended a service at nearby St. John's Church. On these days I stayed away from school for the entire day. Needless to say, I was an object of curiosity to my fellow pupils.

Father never explained why I was isolated from the rest of the school during school assemblies and I never asked, because I had been brought up to accept his decisions without question. However, I learned later that my parents had been in trouble with the local Brethren leaders for sending me to a church based school. I overheard father telling mother, "We are called to be apart". The Brethren said they would withdraw their objections provided I was not allowed to participate in the school's religious activities. After his talk with the Headmaster, father was able to reassure the Assembly's Elders.

For some reason I was allowed to attend Scripture lessons. I rather excelled at these. No doubt this was due to the fact that father read at least one chapter of the Bible to us at the end of each evening meal. Incidentally, it was during Scripture lessons that I harboured the first guilty secret that I chose to hide from my parents. During these lessons our teacher used books that featured pictures of Jesus and other Biblical characters. I knew the Brethren did not approve of such pictures so I kept quiet about them. I remember the feeling of dread in case my guilty secret should ever be discovered. There was one occasion when I did slip up. Towards the end of the year, during a Scripture lesson, we all had a go at making a Christmas calendar. When I took the calendar home my parents were rather upset because the Brethren did not recognise or approve of religious anniversaries such as Christmas or Easter.

In our first year at school we were expected to have a nap during the first half hour after lunch and the blinds in the classroom were pulled down to encourage this.

A favourite stopping off point on the way home from school was our neighbourhood corner shop. If we did not have any money we were content just to look at the sweet jars lined up in the window and watch from the open door as the aproned grocer scooped, weighed and bagged his customers' orders for sugar, flour, lentils and rice. I was particularly fascinated by the way he used a wire-cutter to divide a whole cheese into roughly equal portions. When one of these was selected, the grocer weighed and deftly wrapped it into a neat white package.

On the rare occasion that we had a couple of coppers (large copper pennies) to spend, we took ages before exchanging them for a carefully selected assortment of sweets. Tuppence would buy a packet of lemon sherbet powder, a carton of five sweet cigarettes, two gobstoppers, two aniseed balls, two acid drops, a lollipop and half a dozen hard toffees. We loved gobstoppers because they lasted half an hour and as you sucked away at them they changed colour at least five times. The sherbet cost a quarter of a penny (a farthing) but it was worth it because as you sucked its powder through a black liquorice tube there was a delicious fizz as the mouth's taste buds foamed into life. Incidentally the farthing was Britain's smallest coin and aptly portrayed the wren, this country's smallest bird.

Occasionally, when father was working on Saturday afternoons, mother would take us on a penny tram ride to Abbey Park where we paddled up to our knees in a large, murky looking pond. As the pond was fed by a stream, it was teeming with life. We took empty jam jars and nets made from pieces of lace curtain or old hankies. When these were tied to the end of sticks, we fished for sticklebacks, minnows and tadpoles. Before setting off home, we placed slimy green stuff at the bottom of the jar to keep our captive fish alive. To prevent them escaping, we screwed on a perforated lid. In the days that followed, we kept a careful eye on the fish until the water became too opaque to see them properly.

In my second and third years at school, mother entrusted me with the exact money and a tin to get paraffin at an ironmonger's shop on the main road nearest to our home. The shop always bustled with activity and there was not enough room to wander around. The inside was cluttered with sacks of dog biscuits, corn pellets for birds, along with feed for chickens and rabbits. There were bins holding assorted sizes of nails and screws. These were weighed and handed out to the customer screwed up in a page of newspaper. Amongst the garden tools, mops and brushes were heaps of firelighters. Scores of buckets, saucepans and hurricane lamps hung down from wooden beams in the ceiling. There was also a basket on the counter full of enamel mugs and pottery cups at tuppence a time. Having caught the eye of the ironmonger or his young assistant, my tin would be taken and refilled from a drum of paraffin in the yard at the back. I distinctly remember the ironmonger's shop having its own unique blend of sounds and smells.

During those five years in primary and junior school, I learnt to read and write but found arithmetic more difficult. In spite of this I was made class monitor during the final term. The duties involved giving out and collecting the lesson books. I also had to fill up the desk ink wells. This promotion gave my rather fragile self-confidence a great boost. My final school report included a comment to this effect.

The day for which some of us had been preparing finally arrived. Twelve of us, who had passed the necessary qualifying tests, nervously waited at the door of the classroom reserved for the 'eleven plus' exams. A notice on the door read, 'Quiet - Scholarship Examination in Progress'. We found several rows of desks and chairs awaiting us. It was quite an intimidating experience. Each desk was supplied with two steel-nibbed dip pens, a bottle of black ink, sheets of blotting paper and a ruler.

When the results eventually came through, the Headmaster announced, in Morning Assembly, that of the twelve who sat the examination, three had been awarded scholarships. Two candidates achieved first class passes which qualified them for free entry to one of Leicester's three Grammar Schools. I had been awarded a second class scholarship and this entitled me to attend the City's only Intermediate School. Not being present at School Assembly, I was later told of my pass by a teacher. She explained that the syllabus at an Intermediate School was less academic than at a Grammar School and provided more instruction in craft subjects such as woodwork, metalwork and bicycle maintenance. I think my parents were quietly proud when I told them of my partial success.

# Chapter 5 - Preparing for War

During my final year at St. John's Junior School, preparations for the Second World War were well advanced. The children thought it was great fun, little realising how our lives, to a lesser or greater extent, would be affected by such a war.

The real seriousness of it all came home to us the day we were each issued with a gas mask. They came in square cardboard boxes with strings attached, to allow them to be carried around our necks. The day after we received the masks the whole school was summoned to the hall. A uniformed man, who was introduced to us as a Civil Defence Officer, demonstrated how we were to put on our masks. I remember that the whole exercise generated a great deal of noise and excitement. We were to carry the masks at all times but only wear them when instructed to do so. There were 'black marks' for leaving our masks at home. Thereafter, we had regular gas mask drills and got used to the rubbery smell.

Other reminders of the imminence of war included the precautions being taken against bomb blast. Sandbags were stacked against the schools outside walls and the windows were criss crossed with strips of brown paper. The school basement was to be used as a gas proof air raid shelter and we practised evacuating classrooms in the shortest possible time.

Britain's pre-war Prime Minister, Neville Chamberlain, wrongly thought that he had secured 'peace in our time' for the country, when he was deceived by Hitler into signing the Munich Agreement. As the weeks went by there was no doubting the continuing hostile aims of the Nazi regime in Germany and the threat of war was growing more insistent every month. All hope of peace disappeared when German troops invaded Poland in the summer of 1939. Authorities in Britain predicted that massive air raids would probably take place immediately following the outbreak of war. It was subsequently revealed that nearly forty million gas masks had been issued to the civilian population by the middle of 1939.

It was about this time that I made a deliberate decision to respond to the claims of Jesus Christ, by submitting both my heart and life to God. Very simply I accepted the Gospel invitation that because God loved me, He offered forgiveness and eternal life to all those who came to Him with true repentance and simple faith. The actual moment of decision came during the closing hymn following a Gospel sermon in our Brethren Meeting Room. To be honest, I was inwardly critical of the sermon. For instance, the preacher did not say anything that I had not heard hundreds of times before. I was embarrassed at the way his voice quavered with emotion during the parts of the sermon that most deeply affected him. It was not, however, what we children irreverently called, 'a tear jerker'.

Although I experienced none of the splendid feelings I had expected, the impact of his message had its effect on me. I clearly recall the sense of relief that I had done it at last. The most wonderful realisation of peace and forgiveness replaced the two fears that had previously haunted me. Firstly, that Jesus Christ would come back and find me unprepared to stand before Him on the Day of Judgement. Secondly, preachers warned us repeatedly that we were in danger of becoming 'Gospel hardened' and I did not like the sound of that at all. Years later I read *The Hound of Heaven* by Francis Thompson and this couplet seemed to exactly reflect the feelings I experienced at this crucial juncture in my spiritual life:

*"I fled Him, down the nights and down the days;*
*I fled Him, down the arches of the years".*

As was usual on a Sunday evening, father took me back on the homemade wooden seat he had strapped to the crossbar of his heavy black Raleigh bike. We always dismounted on the steep hill halfway from the Meeting Room to our home. As we puffed our way past the cemetery gates, I plucked up courage to tell my father of the step of faith I had taken earlier that evening. Father was badly crippled as the result of a teenage accident. Despite this handicap, he danced a jig of joy on the pavement and clapped his hands at the same time, with equal vigour. As I think of it now, it was a sort of standing still dance. I never had a really close relationship with my father but for the remainder of that uphill climb, he silently wrapped an affectionate arm around my shoulder.

When we reached the row of Alms houses at the top of the hill, father went into his regular routine. He leaned his bike against the post that held the Request Stop for electric trams travelling from the city centre. Holding out his big black Bible he shouted texts at the top of his voice to the unseen, elderly residents in the Alms houses across the road. Normally I was embarrassed by my father's open air preaching and when people passed by I tried to disassociate myself from him. On this occasion it was different!

When I look back on my years at St. John's School, I have one regret. Although I made some good friends at school, I felt the hardest rule was the Brethren inspired prohibition on the visits of these friends to our home. I was equally disappointed that they forbade my acceptance of repeated invitations to visit their homes. I still had these regrets despite my recent conversion experience. My parents had a clear sense of what they judged to be morally right and wrong, but insisted that there were some things that you just did not do. They did not bother to rationalise why you did not do such things as listening to the radio, reading newspapers, wearing make-up, astrology, smoking, playing cards, drinking and as I said earlier, making friends outside Brethren circles. I remember that the Brethren used to condemn playing cards as The Devil's Pictures and strong drink as Satan's Brew. If mother caught us playing games or even whistling on the Lord's Day she would gently reprove us with the question, "Have you forgotten what day it is?". We did not resent this because we shared our parents' sincere respect for the first day of the week.

# PART 2 - THE SECOND WORLD WAR

The Fear children

# Chapter 6 - Britain at War

The period immediately following the formal declaration of war on 3rd September 1939 proved to be something of an anti-climax. The air raids and gas attacks, which had been predicted to take place in the early weeks of the war, failed to materialise and this caused the early months of the conflict to be known as the phoney war.

One early development that caused a temporary stir was the arrival of children who had been evacuated from London's East End. The evacuees were readily identifiable by the name-tags in their buttonholes, their ragged clothes, pinched faces and strange Cockney accents. Some of these children were billeted in homes while others were put up in schools, public halls and even in churches.

After a few months, most of the evacuees grew increasingly homesick and as there had been no air-raids on London, they gradually returned home, to the great relief of their parents. Meanwhile, the first blackout regulations came into force in 1940, the year in which Winston Churchill became Britain's Prime Minister at the age of 65. The regulations meant that street lights were never lit, car headlights were illegal and lighted windows had to be covered with thick black curtains. We were fortunate to have an indoor Morrison Shelter. The shelter was simply a heavily reinforced steel table under which the whole family could sit during an air-raid. It was not strong enough to protect the occupants in the event of a direct hit but it was designed to withstand structural damage caused by nearby bomb blasts.

We made the shelter as comfortable as possible with a mattress at one end and a paraffin heater at the other. Most of our neighbours had to do with an Anderson Shelter - a trench that was hastily dug by civil defence workers in their back garden. The trench, which quickly became wet and muddy, was then covered with a corrugated iron roof and a thick layer of earth that served both as camouflage and a blast proof protection. Heavy rain made the place thunderously noisy; the din was appalling, allowing little sleep for the occupants. Some of the posher shelters were brick lined and lit by hurricane lamp. The Anderson and Morrison shelters were both named after senior ministers in the wartime government.

As already remarked, the early months of the Second World War were not fought in the air. The media had prophesied that a hurricane of bombs would fall upon London. In the event no bombs threatened the British capital and because of this Churchill warned the people against the danger of being lulled into what he called a 'sinister trance'. There was, however, plenty of action on land and at sea. Germany was sowing magnetic mines in the English Channel which blew up ships passing over them. The Royal Navy tried to sweep the shipping lanes clear while British aircraft were on the lookout for enemy submarines.

In June 1940, over 300,000 servicemen of the BEF (British Expeditionary Force) were hastily evacuated from the beaches of the French seacoast city of Dunkirk. Their rescue was hailed as a miracle. However, with the advance of Nazi troops through France, the British people feared the worst of all possible threats, an imminent invasion of South East England by enemy forces. This perceived threat led to the mobilisation of a million men to the ranks of the Home Guard (formerly known as the Local Defence Volunteers).

The invasion scare provided the background to one of Winston Churchill's most inspiring and historic speeches; the one that ended with the words, "We shall defend our Island, whatever the cost may be. We shall fight on the beaches, we shall fight on the landing grounds, we shall fight in the fields and in the streets, we shall fight in the hills, we shall never surrender." The effect of Churchill's leadership and imperishable words were partly responsible for the preservation of our freedom and democracy, which could have been surrendered but for his courage and eloquence.

Steps were taken by the authorities to negate the threat of any possible enemy invasion. Arms were removed from signposts, milestones on the roadside disappeared and the names on village shops and churches were painted out. Posters began to appear with slogans such as: CARELESS TALK COSTS LIVES, DO NOT BELIEVE RUMOURS AND DO NOT SPREAD THEM and the more enigmatic warning, KEEP MUM - SHE'S NOT SO DUMB. Coastal defences were strengthened with barbed wire fences and concrete pill boxes were built along the 200 mile long south coast. Tree trunks were placed across country lanes to impede the enemy's progress. Despite these precautions, rumours were rife that German parachutists and troop-filled gliders had been seen descending from the skies. Those convicted of spreading such rumours were liable to a term of imprisonment. In the event of an invasion, local authorities were responsible for the ringing of church bells in the area where enemy troops had been spotted.

The long awaited air offensive began in August 1940. It later became known as the Battle of Britain. Strange as it may seem, the action in the air was a relief after the boredom and apathy induced by the phoney war. The air battle began when the German Air Force (the Luftwaffe) launched hundreds of daylight bombing raids on strategic military targets such as British aircraft factories, radar stations, airfields and dockyards. The RAF (Royal Air Force) carried out retaliatory raids that had a devastating impact on German centres of war production and power plants. Both air forces suffered horrendous losses of aircraft and crews during their daylight raids. There were, however, some civilising influences on both sides of the bitter conflict. For example, Germany agreed not to bomb Britain's historic university cities of Cambridge and Oxford if RAF planes refrained from air-raids on similar university cities within its territory.

The direction of the Battle of Britain changed radically in September when German planes made indiscriminate nightly raids on civilian areas of London. Whole streets in the East End were mercilessly destroyed and six incendiary bombs fell on Buckingham Palace, one missing the King and Queen by only thirty yards. The RAF retaliated with a massive campaign of night-time bombing aimed at German cities. The aim of both sides was to knockout their opponent's war machines but sadly the raids slaughtered countless civilians. Most devastated were the cities of Dresden and Coventry which were razed to the ground in great firestorms. In November 1940 German bombers almost completely destroyed the centre of Coventry. The bombers passed over the city for most of the night and left hundreds of corpses lying amongst the rubble. Churchill soon arrived in the city in an attempt to give succour to the survivors by his presence.

Later in the War, the British War Cabinet endorsed the blanket aerial bombardment of citizens in German cities. Three hundred and fifty thousand civilians were killed in one night's bombing of Dresden. British churchmen condemned the aerial offensive on moral grounds. They argued that it offended the moral principle that mankind is responsible for monitoring warfare where diplomacy has failed. Following the evacuation at Dunkirk and the Battle of Britain, something of the ferocity of war came home to us. We began to see wounded troops strolling aimlessly around the centre of Leicester. They were dressed in the regulation military hospital uniform of red, white and blue. This entitled them to free public transport plus admission to entertainment and sporting venues. Some of the troops walked with the aid of crutches and quite a number of them had a trouser leg or arm sleeve pinned up, showing that they had lost a limb in the fighting. It was rumoured, halfway through the war, that convalescent or newly recruited troops needed to have a double rupture or a wooden leg before the authorities would exempt them from active service. The call-up was extended to men up to the age of 50.

The first real victory for allied troops on the ground came in the Middle East at the end of 1942. At El Alamein in Egypt the combined forces of Germany and Italy were defeated by the offensive of the allied forces. Winston Churchill, fearing a let up in the war effort after this success, warned in a broadcast, "This is not the end. It is not even the beginning of the end. But it is", he conceded, "perhaps the end of the beginning". As the War entered its third year the naval conflict in the Atlantic was still going badly. Men, who were previously in reserved occupations, such as teachers, were called up for active service. Their places were taken, for the duration of the war, by teachers coming out of retirement. The continued massive loss of merchant shipping led to further shortages in the UK. White bread, clothes and soap were, in consequence, added to the growing list of commodities already rationed.

Perhaps the most significant civic event of 1942 was the publication of the Beveridge Report. The Parliamentary Committee, headed by Sir William Beveridge, produced the Beveridge Plan which outlined the basis of the future Welfare State. Recommendations included a comprehensive and free health service, generous child allowances, improved old age pensions and the restoration of full employment. In short the Beveridge Report attacked the five giants of Want, Disease, Ignorance, Squalor and Idleness. There was also provision in the Beveridge Plan for the supply of free milk or orange juice to children attending school. The Report's prescription for cradle to grave social security was not, of course, implemented until Clement Atlee's post-war Labour administration was voted into power in 1945.

On the home front all sorts of factories and warehouses were requisitioned for the manufacture of munitions, military vehicles and aircraft. Most of these factories were staffed by women recruited to replace male workers who had been enlisted for military service. Units of the Army's Pioneer Corps were temporarily based in cities. Their task was to dismantle all non-essential iron railings and gates. These were then melted down and used in the manufacture of munitions. The soldiers also collected spare aluminium pots and pans for the manufacture of fighter aircraft.

As anyone who lived through the Second World War will testify, there was a great wartime spirit. The austerities caused by the strict rationing of food, clothes, cosmetics and petrol produced what one writer described as, "the camaraderie of shared discontent". However, it was during this period that I developed a strong and lifelong aversion to Marmite. As it was off the ration, we were served with excessive quantities of thickly spread Marmite sandwiches.

On D-Day, 6th June 1944, allied troops landed in Normandy and after crossing France they triumphantly swept towards the Rhine. This success brought renewed hope to the civilian population, now weary of war, that the conflict would soon be over. We had grown accustomed to seeing American and Commonwealth troops in the streets and their participation in the sweep through Western Europe proved decisive in the eventual defeat of Germany, eleven months later. The morale of the people was also lifted by the arrival of supplies from America. The aid was carefully targeted and helped fill many thousands of empty stomachs.

Although we did not have a wireless set at home, we heard the good news at school. King George and Winston Churchill broadcast to the British people the long awaited news that Germany had surrendered on 4th May 1945 and that the European War was finally over. Both leaders paid tribute to those who had fallen and reminded the nation that it was their sacrifice that had secured victory for Britain and her allies. A columnist, writing for The Observer newspaper two days before Germany officially surrendered on 8th May 1945, identified four things that saved Britain from defeat: "The English Channel, the combined prowess of the Navy and RAF, Mr. Churchill's leadership and the fourth was something in the national character which refused to take in the staring prospect of defeat". We were sad that the Mercy of God was not acknowledged in The Observer article.

The cost of the War, in human terms, had been enormous. It was true that Britain lost far fewer men in World War 2 than in World War 1 (300,000 dead against 750,000) but civilian casualties were higher (60,000 against 1,500). Part of the legacy of the War was a crippling economic debt plus the loss of an Empire. If the war years brought unprecedented hardship to civilians they also brought many benefits. Because of full employment along with fairer distribution of food supplies, poorer families enjoyed a better standard of living than ever before. Price controls also helped to keep the rise in prices within limits. The War proved that full employment was not an impossible dream and with the industrial leap forward, voters were soon to demand, through the ballot box, a fairer social order after the War.

All workers and school children were given a day's holiday to celebrate VE (Victory in Europe) Day on the 8th of May 1945. In recognition of VE Day the rather drab street of terraced houses, where we lived in Leicester, was transformed overnight. Our neighbours produced long ladders and between them they strung up a series of colourful banners across the street. Union Jack flags, gay pennants and balloons hung from the banners high above our heads and many doors were decorated with gaudy coloured crepe paper. An upright piano was pushed out from one house into the middle of our street. Halfway through the afternoon, a variety of tables appeared and scores of parents and children tucked into sandwiches filled with lashings of salted dripping, jam and cheese. When these were eaten jellies, macaroon cakes, buttered slices of malt bread and lemonade appeared on the tables. Mahogany coloured tea was served continuously from a steaming urn with a built in calor-gas heater.

Although we were not allowed to take part in any of the street parties, we observed the non-stop celebrations, in a clandestine sort of way, from our parents' front bedroom window. As it grew dark, the blackout curtains were torn down from windows all along the street. For the first time in five years the pavements were flooded with light. The revellers danced to the accompaniment of the old, out of tune, honky-tonk piano. Bonfires were lit in the nearby park and on the allotments. We also heard the distant peal of church bells and the sound of fireworks. Everyone seemed to be waving flags and as the evening wore on an impromptu procession formed and weaved all over the street. Groups of neighbours held hands and danced in circles to the music of the piano, swaying as though in a hypnotic trance. Younger children sat on the doorsteps watching the dancing and eating lemon curd and peanut butter sandwiches from plates in their laps. All of these festivities were entirely appropriate because the nightmare of war, that the community had endured for so long and with such fortitude, was at long last over.

The war in the Pacific also ended, in August 1945, after allied bombers dropped two devastating atomic bombs. The terrors of modern warfare were unleashed as a means of shortening the War, which was already virtually won. The Japanese cities of Hiroshima and Nagasaki were shattered in the two nuclear raids. Altogether Japan lost over a million servicemen and a quarter of a million civilians during the course of a war that they had started by bombing American naval ships based at Pearl Harbour. After the surrender of Japan the country's Emperor renounced his divine reign and was replaced by his American victor, General Douglas MacArthur. Having lived through that period, I am now struck by the sheer mediocrity of the 'baddies': Hitler, Mussolini and Emperor Hirohito; and the heroic stature of the 'goodies': Churchill, DeGaulle and to a lesser extent, General Dwight Eisenhower. Sir Winston Churchill will always be remembered for his cigar, V-sign, homburg hat, brandy glass, safari suit and of course, his inspiring oratory.

After almost six years of war, Britain's return to peacetime conditions required a long period of adjustment. Despite the remarkably united and disciplined war effort, the country's economy was in poor shape. Although the country was ranked as one of the Big Three post-war powers, it soon became clear that Britain was not in a position to make the same economic contribution as its post-war partners, the Soviet Union and the United States of America. American food parcels, after the war, provided recipients with such delicious things as chocolate bars, crystallised pineapple rings, peanut butter and, of course, sticks of Wrigley's chewing gum.

To retrace the sequence of this narrative, I need to go back to the middle of 1940 when I began four happy years at Moat Road Intermediate Boys' School and this deserves a chapter to itself.

# Chapter 7 - Intermediate School

I failed to realise, until years later, how much my parents sacrificed in order for me to take advantage of the scholarship that entitled me to an Intermediate School education. I look back on those four years at Moat Road Intermediate Boys' School with immense pleasure, for which I was insufficiently grateful to my parents at the time.

In the summer holidays, between my junior and senior schools, father received various letters from the City of Leicester Education Department. I was rather proud to be the subject of such official looking correspondence. One letter specified the gents' outfitter from which my school uniform should be purchased. The uniform consisted of blazer and badge, long trousers, socks, cap with badge, apron for woodwork or metal work and a leather satchel. Another letter advised that, because of my family's low income, we qualified for a grant of £25 a year toward the cost of school dinners. I was also to be given daily doses of cod-liver oil to make up for the vitamin deficiencies caused by the continuing rationing of nutritious food. As my new school was two miles from home I made a small contribution, from my savings, towards the cost of a second hand bicycle.

It was a red letter day for the whole family when, after all the preparations, I nervously cycled across Leicester for my first day at Moat. I remember feeling stiff and self-conscious in my school blazer, my first long trousers and shining black shoes. Mother had not been able to afford a leather satchel so, as a substitute, I hung an old cloth bag on the handlebars of my bike. On that first day at school, mother gave me a paper bag containing four neat square sandwiches of white bread, filled with salted dripping and thin slices of cucumber. She intended these for lunch but I was so hungry I ate the sandwiches during playtime. On my way home from school I occasionally bought a packet of Smith's crisps to assuage my hunger. The paper bag was inscribed 'Founded 1922 at Brentford' and contained a small blue envelope of salt.

After St. John's, Moat presented a more threatening environment to my eleven year old eyes. My first impression of the school was that it consisted entirely of 350 big and rumbustious boys. To answer questions you stood up and you always called the teacher Sir or Miss. I also noted that the classroom walls were all painted in two identical colours. The bottom half of the walls were dark green and the top half was painted cream. External windows were all criss crossed with strips of brown paper to minimise the effects of bomb blasts. The classrooms had cracked lino on the floor and plywood doors with peeling paint. The lavatory block, which we used during playtime, was across the asphalt playground. Its drains were frequently blocked and the overflowing waters were distinctly unpleasant.

The exterior of the school was showing its age with crumbling brick walls and fading paint on windows and walls. Apparently the school building had been scheduled for demolition following the First World War but the building of new factories for Imperial Typewriters and Freeman, Hardy and Willis (the well-known shoe manufacturers) increased the need for school places in the area. The new factories also provided much needed employment for the few military personnel that survived World War 1. Hence, the Moat school buildings were not rebuilt. During the Second World War these factories were requisitioned by the Ministry of Defence for the manufacture of munitions and aircraft.

During the twice weekly School Assembly, the first form boys sat in the front rows of the hall. I came to like the Moat school song, the hymn written by John Bunyan, which was sung to a rousing marching tune:

*"He who would valiant be - 'Gainst all disaster,*
*Let him in constancy - Follow the Master,*
*There's no discouragement - Shall make him once relent,*
*His first avowed intent - To be a pilgrim."*

Everything at the new school took some getting used to but the biggest eye opener, for me at least, was the School Library. The teacher who introduced me to the treasures of the Library was the English Language Master. He was especially good because he was skilled at communicating to us his personal enthusiasm for the subject. Such was this teacher's influence over me that I copied, as near as I could, his rather florid style of joined-up handwriting.

One day he took our class on a guided tour of the School Library and urged us to use its facilities at lunchtimes and during free periods. I did not need any encouragement to spend my free times in the Library. An exciting new world opened up to me through which I could escape the restraints imposed at home and by the Brethren. Not least in this new world was the discovery of comics. The only literature I had been allowed to read at home was aimed at improving our characters. The nearest we came to comics were Brethren periodicals with titles such as, *Joyful News, Wonders of Creation, The Signpost and The Beacon Light.*

Father's bookshelf space was given over almost entirely to the published ministry of Brethren leaders. These included the 37 volumes of *The Collected Writings and Letters* of the founder of the Exclusive section of the movement, John Nelson Darby. However, to be fair, there was one book at home that I cherished and it held my attention for hours on end. It was an odd volume from Arthur Mee's *Children's Encyclopaedia* and turned me into an expert on subjects that began with the letter "M". With the help of this book I became quite knowledgeable on the Magna Carta, military regiments and mining.

It was the world of comics in the School Library that really caught my imagination. Before long I entered the fantasy world of *The Rover, Boy's Own, The Wizard and The Hotspur*. The effect of these comics on an impressionable eleven year old was amazing. The School Library also introduced me to *Picture Post* plus such works of fiction as Arthur Ransome's *Swallows and Amazons* and Buchan's *39 Steps*.

This reminds me that there were several school activities which I kept secret from my parents, for fear of upsetting them. They knew nothing about my love of comics or that the Darwinian theory of evolution was taught by our Biology mistress as a scientific fact, rather than as any other contemporary myth. I also kept quiet about my participation in the two winter sports in which Moat specialised, rugby football and cross country running. I loved sports so much that I even grew to like the smell of the school's changing room with its combination of linseed oil and the reek of perspiration.

My growing prowess in sports came to my parents' attention when they received the report at the end of my first year at Moat. The Games Master said, "John is a most promising rugby player" and predicted, "In due course he will also represent the school at long distance running." Father was troubled about the implication of these comments because, as he warned me, they suggested that

I was becoming more closely associated with teachers and boys than the Brethren allowed. Nevertheless, on the whole he was reassuring and pleased that I was applying myself to what he regarded as serious subjects. He acknowledged that I had done well to come top of the form in English and Scripture. At the end of the second year at Moat, my Form Master said in the Midsummer Term Report, "He has done wonderfully well as Bank and Registration Monitor".

As I look back on those years at Moat, I had several good memories but one that was distinctly unpleasant. It came quite early when, during Morning Assembly, a boy was caned in front of the whole school. The Headmaster announced, in a grave voice, that the boy had been caught in the act of bullying a pupil who was two years younger than himself. I remember wincing as the Games Master gave the hapless boy two hefty strokes on each of his outstretched hands. The offender did not utter a whimper but I was shaken by the violence of such a ritualised beating, even though it served as an effective deterrent for potential bullies in the school. However, the boy who was caned was boasting only days later to having marks on his hands. I can also remember one lady teacher who clouted boys around the ears if she thought they were being less than courteous to her.

Amongst my most enjoyable memories at Moat were the times we spent whole weeks as members of potato picking teams at farms in the Leicestershire and Rutland countryside. Farm labourers had been called up for military service and the help of school children was welcomed by farmers during the autumn harvests. It was a fantastic experience for me. We travelled to and from the allotted farm in a single decker bus (these were known as char-a-bancs). The bus journeys introduced me to the most convivial atmosphere I had ever known. It was quite different from the school classroom. For instance, pupils from the Girls' School joined us and we sang quite racy popular wartime songs. These included, *Pack up your troubles in the old kit bag*; *Oh, I do like to be beside the seaside*; *When I'm cleaning windows*; *Show me the way to go home*; *We'll meet again, don't know where, don't know when*; *It's a long, long way to Tipperary* and *Doing the Lambeth Walk*. I did not know the meaning of most of the lyrics but I really caught on to the catchy tunes. The potato picking was back breaking work. A rather primitive tractor or a Clydesdale horse pulled behind it a wooden agricultural implement, called a potato riddle, that clumsily turned over the roots of the potato plants. We were then left to collect the crop of potatoes. These were piled into wicker baskets that one member of the team took away and tipped into the nearest lorry patrolling the field.

It always seemed an age until lunchtime but when it eventually arrived the wait was worthwhile. One of the farmer's pigs had been killed to provide us with meat for the rest of the week, either served hot as pork chops or cold as cooked ham. One day we had faggots which were made by the farmer's wife from the pig's offal. On the last day of the week we were served with Spam - a pressed meat of unknown origin that came out of catering sized tins. (I later heard that a tribe of ex-cannibals had developed an insatiable appetite for Spam). Strangely, in view of the work we were doing on the farm, we were served with scoops of cooked dehydrated potatoes! I do not know where the tinned pineapple came from, but it was a welcome change from the semolina and tapioca puddings we usually had at school dinners. I went on these potato picking trips for two years in succession, when I was 12 and 13.

During those hilarious weeks I shed a lot of the inhibitions that I had inherited from my strict religious background.

In my last year at Moat I was appointed to act as a school prefect. In this position I was expected to assist the teaching staff with the enforcement of discipline and to report cases of bullying during playtime. All school books had to be covered in brown paper and prefects had the job of reporting boys whose books were dog-eared. I had the extra duty of accompanying the Head Girl from the Girls' School on a weekly inspection of the school's air-raid shelter. This was shared by both schools in the basement. The shelter was cold and dark but spacious. I looked forward to my weekly assignation and possibly for the first time I became aware of the attractiveness of the opposite sex. I remember stealing a kiss on her cheek before she left with her family for their new home in Plymouth.

This could not have been too much of a distraction though because I was awarded a prize on the final speech day. The book, which was presented by the Headmaster, who presided magisterially on such occasions, was entitled *The China General*. It was inscribed in the unmistakable handwriting of my mentor, the English Language Master, "For public service to the School". I have never been more proud of anything, before or since! Unfortunately, not a single member of the Fear Family was present at the most important day of my school life - the final prize giving ceremony.

# Chapter 8 - Father's War

Towards the end of the second year of the War, father received his call-up papers for military service. In keeping with Brethren tradition, he registered as a conscientious objector - a CO or Conchy. (This was the derogatory term used for a person who refused to take up arms on principle.) In due time, father was summoned to appear before a tribunal and had to give evidence as to why he should be granted exemption from service in the armed forces.

Tribunal members were 'worthies' from the local community and they possessed similar sentencing powers to a magistrate's court. They not only examined the applicant's case but also called on witnesses to testify to the sincerity and character of the CO. Parliament granted a wide range of options to these tribunals. They could, for instance, give the appellant a prison term for the duration of the war, instruct them to work down a coal mine or serve in the army in a non-combatant capacity. The authorities subsequently decided who would join the NCC (Non-Combatant Corps) or serve with the RAMC (Royal Army Medical Corps). The prison sentence was usually reserved for politically motivated pacifists and the other options to CO's who pleaded that their objection stemmed from religious convictions.

Before giving their decision, the tribunal ordered that my father should be examined by a Medical Board. Because of his injured leg, which caused my father to walk with a pronounced limp, the Board gave him a 'D' grade. As this ruled him unfit for the armed forces the tribunal instructed him to report to local CD (Civil Defence) officials. They decided that he was fit enough to discharge the duties of an ARP (Air Raid Precautions) Warden. He was duly kitted out with the appropriate uniform and issued with a steel helmet, special ARP Warden's gas mask, stirrup pump, whistle, heavily shaded torch and a first aid kit. His duties included giving assistance to firefighters and bomb disposal experts, especially in rescuing victims of bombing raids. One of his routine tasks was to spot and deal with any breaches of blackout regulations.

The population was warned of an impending air attack by an alert, a siren that rose and fell in pitch. In due course this was followed by a single note siren that indicated the end of an air raid. During raids the wardens were required to patrol the rooftops in their allocated areas to look for incendiary bomb fires and premises flattened by high explosive bombs. It was amazing, considering my father's disabilities, that he was expected to undertake such arduous wartime duties, but he did and for such exploits he became quite a hero to us children.

One of my favourite TV programmes has always been *Dad's Army,* because the characters are so finely drawn. I met every one of those characters on the streets of Leicester. We even had a 'spiv' who offered us a smell of a banana at a penny a sniff.

The bombing of British cities became known as the Battle of Britain. During blitzes the famous British fighter plane, the Spitfire, engaged with enemy aircraft in spectacular aerial dogfights and those German planes that were not shot down were chased by Spitfires and Hurricanes across the English Channel. The cities were also protected by barrage balloons tethered to the ground by steel cables. Barrage balloons were large, gas filled, whale shaped structures, designed to deter low flying enemy aircraft. Banks of searchlights were installed in the vicinity of cities and during raids their beams pierced the night sky to assist the aim of anti-aircraft gunners. These were Gunners, who were serving in an Army regiment known as the Royal Artillery.

From the early days of the War, petrol was strictly rationed. Only those motorists who were issued with coupons, by virtue of their essential occupations, had access to fuel. Father qualified for a couple of gallons a week because of his disability. He owned a Morris Eight saloon car that had known better days. It boasted a sunshine roof that could be opened by turning a handle inside the car. Father had the irritating and potentially dangerous habit of running out of petrol in the most inconvenient places. For instance, on one occasion, he stalled the car between a pair of tramlines. Before anyone was able to evacuate the car, an approaching electric tram that could not stop in time clattered into us. Undeterred by the remonstrations of the startled tram driver, father calmly adopted his usual routine. He quickly hobbled to the back of the car where he opened the filler cap and poured in a pint of petrol from the Tizer soft drinks bottle he kept in reserve under the driver's seat. He then drove off, quite unconcerned, saying, "It's only a small dent!".

One of the thrills of riding on a Leicester tram was the way it rocked wildly as the driver drove it at seemingly reckless speeds. It squealed along the tracks and appeared to be so out of control that at such times it was too hazardous for passengers to clamber down the spiral stairs from the top deck. This rush to the terminus was in the driver's interest because his job depended on keeping to the timetable should a Corporation Inspector flag down his tram.

Air Raid Wardens had two nights off duty a week. Father did all he could to arrange for these to be on Sundays and Mondays so that he could attend the Brethren meetings, regularly arranged for those evenings. When I was about twelve years old he started to take me with him to the Monday Prayer Meetings. On one of these nights we came out of the Meeting Room at 9 o'clock to find a rosy glow tingeing the sky. Leicester was on fire! Searchlights stabbed into the sky and illuminated the only aerial dogfight I saw during the war. I have always wondered what happened to the two night fighter planes because they only engaged, spitting fire high above us, for a few breath-taking minutes before they disappeared. I was overwhelmed by the courage and dedication of the two fighter pilots.

Rather than taking the risk of being caught up in the bombing, the Prayer Meeting was extended. I remember very clearly hearing, during one period of silence, the hiss as drops of evaporating water fell on the red hot top of the iron coke stove (I think it was called a Tortoise stove) at the back of the Meeting Room. When we looked out of the door several hours later, the sky was bathed in translucent pre-dawn moonlight. The fires had died down and, as the area was blacked out, the whole city was drenched in the moon's glow, with no other lights to detract from its brilliance. Soon the sun mounted the sky and we trudged home wearily, through bombed out streets, to be welcomed home by mother who was extremely anxious, having feared the worst.

# Chapter 9 - Our Allotment

During the war years the German navy sank many thousands of tons of British merchant shipping. As a result there was an acute shortage of food, especially in the urban areas of Britain. Rationing was introduced early in the War and continued for two or three years after it was over. To alleviate the food crisis, Churchill's coalition government launched the successful Dig for Victory campaign. To support this drive for home-grown food, local authorities were given statutory powers to requisition vacant plots of land including, for instance, school playing fields. These plots were allocated to citizens who volunteered to use them for the cultivation of fruit, vegetables and domestic livestock. (The word allotment originally meant: Land allocated to the poor.) Eventually 1.75 million plots were cultivated under the Dig for Victory scheme. On these small plots allotment holders raised a tenth of all the food produced in Britain during the war years. At certain periods of the year packets of free vegetable seeds from America were available from the local Dig for Victory office.

We rented a full size plot which cost my parents £2 a year. It was about a ten minute walk from home but as our allotment had its own lockable shed we could leave our garden tools and wooden wheelbarrow there, together with the back seat of an old car on which we occasionally sat. My brother, Paul, and I were paid a few pence for every bucket of horse manure that we collected on Saturday mornings, so the topsoil of our allotment was in good fertile condition. We found it profitable to follow the milkman who led his horse and cart around our area. We would shovel up any manure that the horse deposited in the streets. Allotments tended to be both scruffy and resourceful at the same time. Sheds and greenhouses were cobbled together from old doors and sheets of corrugated iron. We became accomplished vegetable growers and grew enough in the summer and autumn to feed the whole family. We also extended the growing system by using homemade glass and wire cloches. By this means we grew out of season salad crops such as lettuces, cabbages and carrots.

I said that allotment holders were resourceful. They were also a fraternity who liked to pass on growing hints to each other. Two hints that I remember concerned the growing of potatoes and runner beans. Seed potatoes were very scarce so we saved and planted any potato peelings that possessed one or more eyes. We also over wintered and planted the tubers of runner bean plants. Both these ideas produced rather lower yields than by the more usual method but vegetables grown this way were still most welcome. Mother made jam from the raspberries and gooseberries which she picked from the few soft fruit bushes on the allotment. I cannot remember eating any of the jam because mother had the habit of supplementing the rations of friends who were, in her charitable estimation, needier than ourselves.

A railway line ran past the end of our allotment. We spent many happy hours collecting the names and numbers of the huge locomotives as they picked up steam on their way north or as they let off a warning whistle approaching Leicester station. Paul and I played a slightly daring game that we kept secret from our family. It involved scrambling down the steep embankment so that we could balance a penny on the nearest railway line. When the rail began to vibrate we retreated halfway up the embankment and from there we waved to the passing engine driver. More often than not he or his fireman would wave back. When the last carriage of the train had disappeared through the tunnel we retrieved the penny that was hotter and thinner than before the train's wheels had run over it. We treasured these pennies as much as the pieces of shrapnel we found in the street after an air-raid.

The garden shed on our allotment became a magical place for us children. In retrospect I think it was equivalent to the wardrobe in C.S. Lewis' Narnia stories. The illusion was ruined, however, when we installed a small flock of twelve Rhode Island Red chickens. Father bought these, together with a couple of rabbits, for a total of £3 at Leicester's cattle market. The rabbits escaped from their hastily assembled hutches within a couple of days, never to be seen again! We knew nothing about rearing chickens but the local Dig for Victory office gave father a leaflet on the subject. The chicken feed proved to be an irresistible attraction to rats who gnawed through the back of the shed. Apart from eating the cooked corn, we suspected that the rats also stole the odd egg.

The hens necessitated a daily visit to the allotment. Paul and I took this in turns, except on Sundays. They turned out to be good layers and our visits were rewarded with a regular supply of fresh eggs, sometimes as many as eight a day. Father sold about half of these from his weekly herbal stall in Leicester Market (at the time the largest open air market in Europe) for a penny an egg. The proceeds paid for the regular supply of chicken feed and any balance left over contributed to the family's meagre housekeeping budget. For once father's investment proved to be profitable, not least because fresh eggs were a welcome alternative to dried egg powder, which was not only horrible to taste but rationed as well.

# Chapter 10 - Medical Herbalism

I have already referred to the fact that my father was a Medical Herbalist. As far as I can recall, father was largely dependent for his herbal remedies on herbs that were seasonably plentiful. He was presumably unable to afford dried herbs or tinctures from wholesale suppliers. He gathered basic common herbs from the fields, embankments and woods within cycling distance of our home.

Herbs are humanity's most ancient healing aids with a history of several thousand years of continuous use. Nevertheless, in father's time medical herbalism was not the respectable alternative therapy it is today. The media of his day publicised fraudulent claims of charlatans who practised it and also gave space in the newspapers to criticisms by orthodox medical practitioners. Today, orthodox (allopathic) doctors recognise that leaves, roots, berries and bark, which are used in traditional herbal remedies, are an important source for their therapeutic drugs.

Research laboratories, by isolating the active substances of herbs, tend to increase the incidence of serious and unpleasant side effects by the synthetic manufacture of more powerful drugs than those milder remedies prescribed by herbalists. To treat illness with herbs, an accurate diagnosis is essential. This is because the herbal mixture recommended will be tailor-made to treat the symptoms of the individual patients. Herbalists are also trained to know which herbs would be toxic if prescribed for unsuitable patients or in excessive quantities. The aim of herbal treatment is to nourish the main organs of the body so that they can function to their full capacity. Herbs are not, however, for patients who are impatient and want an instant cure. Unlike synthetic drugs, herbal mixtures contribute to a slower and safer healing process. Good herbal practitioners warn their patients that herbal remedies take a while to show results and they should be willing to take a month's treatment before evaluating its effectiveness.

Father enlisted his first patients by distributing leaflets to homes in the larger villages of Leicestershire. He was once arrested and questioned by the police when one of his leaflets was found in a house that had been burgled. His panel of patients also grew as a result of personal recommendations by those he contacted at his stall in Leicester Market. He regularly visited the homes of patients. This allowed him to make a more accurate diagnosis and review the progress of individuals who had consulted him. Over the years father received hundreds of letters that testified to the efficacy of his herbal treatments. For instance, he made up a simple remedy for treating the common cold, influenza and sore throats. This was made from an infusion, in equal parts, of peppermint, yarrow and elderflower. He kept free of colds himself by eating a raw Spanish onion every day and by seasoning his food with liberal quantities of cayenne pepper. He also chewed cinnamon bark as a preventative measure. For readers with an interest in the subject I will list those herbs that father proved to be effective:

Fresh comfrey leaves (known as boneset) have been used for centuries as a poultice to relieve the inflammation caused by sprains and bruises. It can also be used to treat varicose veins.

The oil from comfrey is used by arthritis sufferers who rub it into affected joints.

Root of valerian has been helpful to those who suffer from sleeplessness.

Camomile provides a relaxing night-cap for insomniacs as well as being effective in the relief of pain.

A mixture of sage, dandelion roots and nettles can be used as a blood purifier and herb tonic.

Basil is an insect repellent.

Marigold flowers help to repel white fly.

Dill seed is a popular remedy for indigestion. It is the active ingredient in gripe water for babies. The seeds are invariably served with the bill at good restaurants in the United States.

Daisy flowers, used as a poultice, are used to treat the broken veins that develop in some people's noses.

Greater celandine plant flowers are prescribed for treating warts.

Sage is a useful gargle for sore throats and sage leaves can be used to clean and polish teeth.

Root of ginger can be used as an antidote against motion sickness caused by road, sea and air travel.

An infusion of dried senna pods is a gentle remedy for the relief of constipation.

Wild parsley is said to be a health giving herb because it is rich in vitamins A, B, C and iron. It also provides relief for rheumatism sufferers.

Herbs are very versatile. In addition to their medicinal properties they have many traditional culinary and cosmetic uses. The basic herbs used in culinary dishes and salads include chives, cumin, fennel, mint, parsley, sage and thyme. At home we kept a fresh supply of these herbs in small pots on the inside of our kitchen window. Herbs have their cosmetic uses as well. For example, an effective moisturising skin cream can be made from carrot root oil or the crushed leaves of aloe vera. Parsley can be used as a deodorant and lavender to add perfume to drying clothes. It is claimed that unpleasant body odours can be killed by adding tomato juice to bath water.

Herbal therapists maintain that it is gentler and safer if the whole herb containing the active ingredient is used, rather than drugs which are manufactured in synthetic form from the active element alone. There is a slight danger of the toxic effect that can occur when herbs are taken in large doses. Having said that, even animals are instinctively aware of the curative powers of various plants. Dogs and cats chew grasses and green leaves to increase their stamina and to remedy various ailments.

About a quarter of modern drugs are derived from plants. These include the invaluable heart drug digoxin, derived from digitalis which is found in the leaves of the foxglove family. Aspirin, which comes from the bark of the willow tree, is effective in the relief of pain, headaches and in the initial treatment of feverish colds and chest infections. A licence was granted in 1992 to drug companies for the experimental use of a drug derived from the bark of yew trees. Researchers are hoping that the bark's active ingredient, Taxol, will prove to have cancer killing properties that will interfere with the mechanism that makes cells divide and so reduce the size of malignant tumours.

Father seems to have learnt his herbalism instinctively rather than from a textbook. He made a frugal living from his herbal practice. His income was barely sufficient to meet the needs of his growing family. This was not helped by his somewhat sanguine attitude to his financial responsibilities. He only charged patients for their remedies if they could afford to pay for them. Many persuaded him that they could not, so they were supplied with herbs free of charge. He was generous to a fault but then frittered away far more than he could afford on a non-essential kitchen gadget or something that took his fancy at Leicester Market. He just could not resist a bargain! The shortage of housekeeping money meant that mother could only afford the cheapest joint of meat, such as neck of lamb, for our Sunday lunch.

During my last year at Moat I was always keen to earn some pocket money. Father paid me half-a-crown (there were eight to the pound) for going to Nuneaton every other Saturday. I took my bike to catch an early train for the twenty mile journey from Leicester to Nuneaton. Before intending passengers paid their fare through the hole in the ticket office window, they could not miss the huge poster at the side of the window. It simply asked the question, IS YOUR JOURNEY REALLY NECESSARY? Along the station platform there were various enamel advertising panels for Reckitt's Blue, Craven A cigarettes, Oxo, Ovaltine, Andrews Liver Salts and Beechams Pills, which the manufacturer claimed were, "worth a guinea a box". I could not help feeling that only wealthy people could afford these pills.

Leicester's London Road railway station had an exciting atmosphere all of its own. The four main passenger platforms were covered by matching, elaborately designed ironwork canopies. These were suspended on a series of square columns. The platforms were reached by identical flights of stone stairs that led from the bustling street-level, booking hall area. On each pair of platforms there was a refreshment room and a gents' lavatory. The station provided four waiting rooms, all ablaze with coal fires. The two ladies' rooms included cloakroom facilities and the other two were for general travellers. At the end of each platform, where train spotters and assorted schoolboys assembled (it cost them a penny platform ticket), there was a water tower. The fireman of each arriving steam locomotive manipulated the huge rubber hose (attached to the water column) into place so as to replenish the water supply in the locomotive's boiler. A man with a lamp and an iron hammer moved up and down the locomotive and carriages tapping the wheels and rails to make sure that they were sound. Before the train was allowed to depart the guard, armed with a green and a red flag, waved the green one to the driver and blew his whistle to confirm the signal. He then boarded the slowly moving train.

It was unfortunate that the railway line, leading to Leicester's main passenger station, was routed through the city's least attractive urban sprawl. It ran between a mile or so of suburban back yards and untended, soot-polluted rear gardens. As a result rail passengers were denied a glimpse of the attractive parks and monuments for which the citizens of Leicester were justly proud.

On my first rail journey I parked my bike in the guard's van, next to a pen of bleating sheep. I then stood nervously by the door of the adjacent corridor. After a while we picked up quite a head of steam and as I was looking out of the open window we travelled through a tunnel. At that moment a train rushed by in the opposite direction. It only seemed to be inches away and the carriage immediately filled with steam and smoke. We were travelling on the LMS (London, Midland and Scottish) railway, on the route between Norwich, Peterborough and Birmingham. The incident must have had the desired effect of scaring the life out of me because I never stuck my head out of the window of a moving train again.

The purpose of my errand to Nuneaton was to collect a hundred rough canvas shopping bags from a 'sweat shop' in the town. These cost father fifty shillings and he sold them from his herbal market stall. Before the bags were ready for sale, mother and father laboriously turned the stiff hand sewn bags inside out. There was very little profit after the cost of the train fare and a proportion of the stall's rent was taken into account.

The acute shortage of funds at home made it necessary for me to leave school a year earlier than was usual for an Intermediate School. The Headmaster was a magistrate and, as if to prove it, he wore a bowler hat and smoked huge cigars. He said he was sorry I was leaving prematurely but he had received a note from my father saying that we needed the extra income to feed the family. I should mention in this connection that Paul had distinguished himself by winning a scholarship to a Grammar School. We were all proud of Paul, as a scholarship boy, but his examination success inevitably added to the pressures on the Fear family budget.

It was during my last term at Moat that I first preached in the open air. The opportunity came when, by my presence, I went to support the weekly gospel witness that was held during lunchtimes in Leicester Market. The service was arranged by members of the city centre Free Church. I really admired their courage and enterprise. When the group's leader stepped down from his platform, I commended him on the message he had just given. He smiled, looked me up and down and said, "Right, you're on next!". This caught me on the hop and as I mounted the stand, I remember the inner turmoil of the moment.

Speaking in public for the first time can be one of life's most terrifying experiences. It is no exaggeration to say that the heartbeat accelerates, the knees buckle, the hands shake, the stomach is agitated and the throat is dry. When I finally opened my mouth all that came to mind was the title of the latest gospel tract that I had read, "If you were to die tonight would you go to Heaven or to Hell?".

This now seems to be a rather finger-pointing question but the few folk who were standing around seemed to be listening. I simply related how I had escaped from my personal fear of death and Hell by turning to Christ who had paid the necessary price for me to enter into Heaven. The preacher who followed me fired a flame-thrower of a sermon that blasted into the small crowd who were listening. Most of them gradually dispersed to escape its heat. I walked away too, having learnt a valuable lesson!

# PART 3 - POST WAR YEARS

John with David and Elizabeth

# Chapter 11 - Leaving School

I left school in July 1945. This was the month that Labour won a surprising landslide victory in the General Election. The Labour Party took office after promising, in their election manifesto, that they would introduce fundamental social and economic reforms. Clement Atlee, a loyal colleague in Churchill's wartime coalition government, was obviously seen by the electorate as the leader best suited to oversee the nation's transition from war to peace and to introduce the radical welfare provisions of the Beveridge Plan. The servicemen's vote was overwhelmingly in favour of Labour.

Close political colleagues of Winston Churchill say that he was devastated by the Conservative Party's defeat in the Election. He interpreted the failure of his bid to lead a peacetime administration as an ungrateful snub by the voters who had, only weeks earlier, acclaimed his outstanding leadership in the Second World War. Political commentators, however, concluded that Churchill was unable to understand the men and women he had led during the war. For instance, in one of his earliest party political broadcasts on the BBC (British Broadcasting Corporation), he patronised the British people by addressing them as, "You, who are listening to me in your cottages".

The popular tabloid press were also influential in bringing about Churchill's defeat in the election. Just when the war-weary working classes were looking for a new social order, one of these newspapers gave prominence to his criticism of the Beveridge Plan in 1943. The paper's political commentator said that Churchill had dismissed Beveridge as, "an awful windbag and a dreamer" and alleged that he doubted the economic wisdom of the proposed post-war reforms.

Before searching for my first job I spent two weeks holiday with the family. Because of the continuing shortage of petrol we spent this time camping in a barn which belonged to a friendly farmer near Coalville, a coal mining town, eight miles from Leicester. It was a hot, glorious summer and we had a barbecue or picnic every day with sweet, milky tea brewed on a bonfire. We spent the days stalking through fields and woods, chasing rabbits, climbing trees, sliding down railway embankments and enjoying catching games with a hard cricket ball.

Father shaved in a nearby stream, using a cut-throat razor and a hogshair shaving brush. Father's paternal family can be traced back to Chew Magna, a village south of Bristol, in the year 1523. I would not be surprised if father had a fair amount of nomadic blood flowing through his veins. He was adept at lighting bonfires, shaving in the stream and foraging for herbs. He never much cared what he looked like. He grew a greying, stubbly chin between shaves. His clothes were always dishevelled and he did nothing to disguise the smell of Spanish onion, which he ate daily to ward off colds.

During this farm holiday I renewed my rather intense friendship with one of the farmer's daughters, Joan. She was my first girlfriend! Joan was 13 and we met on most days, discovering the exquisite pleasure of running barefoot through wet grass. We also spent a lot of time playing and hiding in the acres of gorse and bracken that separated the farm's grazing meadows from the outcrop of granite facing the main Leicester to Coalville road. One day I chiselled on the rock face, in foot high letters, the words, JESUS LIVES. My parents got to know about my youthful attempts at evangelism when I returned to the barn with hands that were bruised and bleeding from such rough treatment. The words were still clearly visible when I travelled past the rocks, in a car, two years later. I only realised then that the defacement of the rock had been an act of vandalism. Perhaps this was an early example of graffiti, but in a good cause!

After our summer holiday I reported to the Employment Exchange. The smoke filled reception area was crowded with recently demobilised servicemen who looked uncomfortable in their demob suits. Much to my surprise I was given an introduction card to the Leicester Royal Infirmary for a job that was described as Junior Clerk. At the same time I was given an appointment to be interviewed by the hospital's Office Manager.

# Chapter 12 - First Jobs

Compared with the teachers at Moat, the Office Manager at the LRI (Leicester Royal Infirmary) was very ordinary. I remember him mainly for the badly frayed collar of his shirt. At the interview he seemed to be in a hurry and after a five minute talk he offered me the job of Office Boy at fifteen shillings (75 pence) a week. I agreed with mother that I would keep a third of this to spend myself.

Work started the following Monday and my duties became clearer by the end of the week. If the rebellious streak in me was awakened during the weeks of potato picking at school, it grew appreciably during my first few months at work. Taking into account my age (15), I was extremely surprised that some of my duties were connected with patients who died in the hospital.

Firstly, I had to contact the last hospital doctor who had treated the deceased and get him to sign the death certificate, entering on it the precise cause of death (I never met a female doctor at the LRI). Secondly, I was required to accompany the next of kin to the mortuary so that they could identify their dead relative. I also had to obtain from them a receipt for the dead person's belongings. Up to this time I had never seen a dead body but now I was seeing two or three a day, something I never quite got used to. I learnt to handle these duties with the sympathy and sensitivity appropriate to the occasion and was often rewarded with a small monetary gift.

I was also surprised to be made responsible for administering the files of patients waiting for admission to the hospital. They were referred for in-patient treatment by the consultants from the out-patient clinics. The waiting lists were divided into three categories - medical, surgical and gynaecological. Waiting list forms on blue sheets were given priority because these patients needed urgent treatment for cancer. Ordinary patients were called into hospital in the order in which they had been placed on the waiting list. The number to whom we offered admission depended on the available bed space. This was notified to the office by the respective Ward Sisters. The only exception to this routine applied to operations for such minor surgical procedures as hernias, tonsils and varicose veins. These cases were held in reserve to fill last minute cancellations caused by the prior death of a patient or people on the waiting list moving out of the hospital's area.

The other regular job that I had at the LRI was to distribute the supply of stationery stocks to the ten wards and various departments within the hospital. This particular job began early on Monday mornings and only ended once the assignment had been completed. It took me two hours to collect all the completed order forms and deliver them to the manager in Stationery Stores. The staff in the stores made up the orders and piled them on two hospital trolleys.

I took out the first trolley immediately after lunch had been served on the wards. As I got to know the ward staff better (especially the student nurses who flattered me with their attentions and offers of coffee), the ward round grew from two to about three hours. I fell in love constantly but it was mostly unrequited. The distribution of stationery to departments was a more hurried affair. I rushed the second trolley around the other hospital departments to allow me to cycle the mile home in time for our evening meal.

At the end of my first year at Leicester Royal Infirmary, I was unexpectedly offered the job of conducting groups of financial donors around the hospital. As the LRI was a voluntary institution, it depended for a substantial part of its income on contributions from supporters. In those days, before the introduction of the National Health Service, patients were means-tested to ensure that they qualified for free treatment.

The two hour tours were arranged for Saturday afternoons and for this duty I was paid half a day's overtime pay. I especially enjoyed it when the people showed a lively interest in the hospital. After a time I gained the confidence to talk convincingly about its work on the basis of the most superficial knowledge. This was certainly the case when we visited the pathology laboratory with its jars of pickled human organs or the operating theatre with its grisly display of surgical instruments.

Apart from the routine spiel, learned from the previous guide, I became quite glib at answering questions from visitors. I included the mortuary in the tour even though it was not listed on the official itinerary. My predecessor had also shown me how to hold open the door, at the end of the tour, to make sure that I received the best possible gratuity. A generous party of twenty could give enough to equal my week's wages but the total tip usually totalled less than ten shillings (50 pence).

If I finished the tour by 4 o'clock I would rush off to Leicester City's football ground, which I could reach in five minutes. The entrance gates were opened at half-time. This allowed me to see most of the second half of the game without having to pay. At the time the Leicester City side were in the second division of the English Football League. I remember that they had a Welsh international player, Dai Jones, who was a great favourite with the crowd. Jones was a full back and his speciality was to gain possession of the ball deep in his own half and to kick it into the opposing teams' penalty area. For me, even on a bad day, Dai Jones could do no wrong. Footballers in the 1940's wore knee length white shorts and cropped hair. To my youthful eyes they all appeared middle aged.

I have already hinted that the early months of my working life marked the period when I kicked over the traces in a big way! My parents would have been shocked had they known that I regularly attended professional football matches and fraternised with student nurses. But, according to the Brethren imposed scale of transgressions, there was a worse sin to come. (Incidentally, I do not relate these examples of my double life with pride but in the interests of truth.) One Saturday afternoon, when Leicester City's scheduled match had been called off, I plucked up the considerable courage needed to go to the cinema. My parents had always held out the prospect of Jesus coming back and catching me in the cinema. Until then that had been a strong enough deterrent!

My introduction to films began when I crept, under the cover of darkness, to a threepenny seat in the middle of the front row of the nearby Regal Cinema. Within the first few minutes I was terrified by the intimidating images of Sherlock Holmes (Basil Rathbone) and the rampaging, snarling Hound of the Baskervilles that reared above me in distorted perspective. All of this was accompanied by the booming soundtrack reverberating around the walls of the cinema.

As my eyes grew accustomed to the gloom I was further discomforted to discover that I was sitting all alone. The nearest patrons were sitting a score of rows behind me in the rear seats. My first visit to the cinema left such an indelible impression on me that I was relieved to leave the Regal, with furtive glances to left and right. There was a certain frisson in these clandestine activities and I hoped, in vain as it happened, that my sins would not find me out.

The discovery of my misdemeanour came about because I was innocently unaware that my clothes and hair had become heavily impregnated by the smell of tobacco smoke in the close confines of the cinema. This meant that after I had hurried home and composed myself outside the house, I was quite unprepared for my father's prescient rebuke, "Son, you've been in the far country", a reference to the parable that Jesus told of the Prodigal Son in Luke's Gospel. When I blurted out my confession that I had been to the cinema, father exiled me to my bedroom, without food, for the rest of the day. My parents appeared in the room a couple of hours later. Both of them were angry, but in a way that those who are really concerned about you are angry. They were close to tears and left me, with no defence, a couple of minutes later. I cried all night.

Although I really enjoyed my work at Leicester Royal Infirmary, I was suddenly sacked from my job there after two years. This was because I had inadvertently broken an unwritten rule that applied to all hospital staff. From early childhood I had suffered frequent recurrences of acute sore throats. Rather than asking my own doctor for the usual referral to the hospital's ENT (Ear, Nose and Throat) specialist, I decided to bypass the system by obtaining an appointment for the out-patient clinic. I was placed on the waiting list and in due course was admitted to a surgical ward for the removal of my tonsils and adenoids. This led to a strong disagreement with my father who objected to all operations that were not absolutely essential. Upon my return to work, after the operation, I was in even more serious trouble. I was summoned to the chandeliered office of the hospital's General Secretary. He sat behind a huge desk and I stood, like a guilty penitent, on the expensive looking carpet in front of him. After his headmasterly rebuke, for my breach of the infirmary's rules, he gave me a week's notice.

Several hours later, still badly shaken, I announced the news at home. My parents took it in their stride, probably interpreting it as an answer to prayer. I guess they thought that my sacking had been providential, because it removed me from those influences that they perceived had begun to lead me in dangerous directions. I had fully expected to stay at the Leicester Royal Infirmary until I was called up, at 18, for two years' mandatory National Service. I fervently looked forward to this as it would give me a legitimate escape route from the restraints of living at home. But the mobilisation was still a year away. As it happened, my two years' experience as a hospital office junior fitted a job vacancy at the *Leicester Mercury* for a Solicitor's Clerk.

The solicitor who took me on was a charming, elderly gentleman who had lost his only son in the war. After a few weeks of answering the telephone, sticking on postage stamps and witnessing wills, he offered to give me free articles. These are equivalent to an apprenticeship and are a prerequisite to sitting the Law Society's examinations. Most solicitors charge a premium for training an articled pupil but, in consideration of my parent's low income, he waived the usual fee of a hundred guineas a year. The articles were to last for five years and I was thrilled to sign up for such an unexpected and promising career. My general office duties did not change much except for occasional visits to the local Magistrates Courts and the preparation of legal documents, such as those used for the conveyancing of property from the vendor to the purchaser.

It was quite a Dickensian office really. My principal had practised there as a solicitor for over thirty years. He wore a wig and gown for his court appearances. He wrote in purple ink with a quill pen and was perpetually covered in cigarette ash as a result of his chain smoking. Shelves in the basement were stacked from floor to ceiling with thousands of parchment deeds and wills. These legal documents, which were tied in pink ribbons, were embossed with red wax seals and government tax stamps. A dozen steel boxes contained documents of the firm's most important clients and the keys to these were locked away in the office safe.

I really enjoyed that year in the solicitors office. It gave me a window into the elite world of the wealthy and privileged members of society. It also awakened within me a desire to study a range of academic subjects in greater depth.

# Chapter 13 - Life at Home

Before describing life in the Army, as a National Serviceman, let me tell you about the Fear family home that I was so keen to leave.

The inside of our home reflected, quite accurately, the frugal lifestyle of our parents. Paul and I shared a bedroom which was sparsely furnished with iron bedsteads, both of which had sagging mattresses. We also had a cheap plywood wardrobe for our clothes. As the window of our bedroom was at the back of the house, we did not have any curtains. The floors downstairs were covered with linoleum and the walls with flower patterned wallpaper.

There were only two pictures on display in our home. One of these was a faded picture of Queen Victoria that hung from a wall above a fireplace. The other was a water colour drawing, in sepia, of Lake Windermere. Several Bible texts, one embroidered, hung on various walls. One said, "Underneath are the everlasting arms". I did not know then what the text meant but it sounded rather reassuring. We also had a scripture calendar on the kitchen wall. Before we left for school mother would tear off a text which she hoped we would memorise during the day.

In addition there was a wind-up gramophone on which we played, among other recordings, a perforated cardboard disc of *Fingal's Cave*. We also had a cardboard record with a laminated surface. It advertised Nestle's chocolates and contained the recordings of several children's poems. The other recording we had was a wax disc with five minutes of bird song on each side. The unfortunate thing about the mechanical gramophone was that it slowed down at the most crucial moments. It was then necessary to crank up the machine to get more music or other sounds out of its big horn speaker.

There was also a wheezy push-pedal harmonium in the front room which gave my mother brief respites from bringing up a large family. Its pedals were covered with pieces of worn carpet. On a couple of evenings a week mother played tunes from her Brethren Hymn Book, *Hymns and Spiritual Songs for the Little Flock*. We grouped around the ancient instrument, singing the words that gave us a very good grounding in Calvinist theology.

The gramophone and organ were the nearest we got to family entertainment. There was of course no radio, television, magazines, newspapers or card games in our strict Brethren home. Father declared that the wireless was nothing but the invention of the devil and he told us the story of a dissident brother who ordered a radio set by post. When it arrived his conscience was stricken by the slogan stencilled on the box, which read, "This radio will bring the world into your home". Father would read from the Bible and before the younger children were sent to bed he led family prayers.

After our evening meal Paul and I took turns doing the washing up. Mother joined us in the kitchen to cook a fresh supply of soda bread. Baker's yeast was scarce during the war but the recipe for soda bread also caused the dough to rise in the oven. Mother brewed regular supplies of ginger beer and dandelion & burdock drinks. She made these drinks from a starter yeast that had been kept alive with sugar for as long as I could remember. It was still necessary, five years after the war, to produce a child's green ration book to be able to obtain two eggs, double the weekly ration for adults. There were just a few items that could be obtained from the butcher without a ration book. These included tinned Snook (a fish of uncertain origin), tripe, vegetable or soya sausages, offal, brawn, black pudding and, of course, beef dripping. If you were a good customer, the butcher would wrap two-pennyworth of bones in a newspaper for making soup or meat stock. Mother did not go to bed until she had laid out all of our clothes, in the order we needed to put them on in the morning, having washed them earlier in the day.

Mother did a daily wash in our kitchen sink. She rubbed a bar of yellow or carbolic soap into the wet clothes before scrubbing them, stretched over a ribbed wooden board. A Reckitt's Blue cube was added to the water used for washing our white shirts and blouses. Eventually the soapy water was drained into a bucket and poured over the back garden plants. A wooden-rollered mangle was used to wring out heavier material such as blankets. These then joined the hand-wrung clothes that were pegged on the clothes line suspended between a hook and a steel pole in the back garden. Mother spent an hour most evenings ironing our clothes. She heated the heavy iron on an iron stand that was placed over glowing embers in the fire. She tested the hot iron either by holding its base close to her cheek or by touching it with a moistened finger. The freshly ironed clothes were hung around an iron mesh fireguard.

Father spent an occasional evening mending our shoes. He used a heavy iron device consisting of a flat base with two foot shaped arms - one large and the other smaller. He slipped a shoe onto the appropriate sized arm. He tacked a leather sole onto the bottom of the shoes to keep our feet warm and dry. Father got his leather supplies from the rejects of a local boot and shoe factory. When he ran out of leather, father substituted it with pieces cut from old bicycle tyres.

Saturday night was bath night. The weekly ritual took place in our zinc bath in front of the living room coal fire. On winter evenings we had to get used to being very cold on one side and uncomfortably hot on the other. Every so often our bath water was replenished with boiling water carried in an enamel jug, topped up from a steaming bucket on top of the gas stove in our kitchen. After ten minutes the latest occupant of the bath gave way to the next oldest bather.

About once a month a black-faced coalman humped a couple of bags, from his horse-drawn cart, to add to the small heap of coal in our outhouse. I rather liked the smell of coal dust that swirled around him.

I think, as I recall life at home, that it was my mother who gave me such a rich and happy childhood. Everything in her life was ordered and she radiated peace to all around her. Although she was worn out from having given birth to eight children, an inadequate diet and her other household chores, she talked enthusiastically about Jesus to everyone she met and was single-minded in her determination to please God. I deeply regret the sorrow we caused her when most of the children later left the Exclusive Brethren and, as she saw it, became apostate by deserting the true Christian path.

It is true, I think, that children can rarely see their parents as others see them, but my impression is that father found it difficult to communicate directly with his children. We were immediately disciplined for any hint of disobedience or lack of respect for mother. I did not really have an affectionate relationship with my father. Although we shook hands, I cannot remember ever kissing or even hugging him, although I must have done as a small child. We disliked the ever present cane that could reach to the furthest of us children at mealtimes. He used the cane lustily, but fairly, on his four sons and left us with a memory that was not really worthy of him, of a harsh Victorian parent. Father was, it seemed to us, someone who was hard to please but easy to enrage. I have to say that father's beatings made a deep impression on me and it took a while for our relationship to recover from his violent eruptions of temper. In common with many other families, our father treated his younger children, James and Mary, with greater moderation.

Having written in a somewhat negative way about my memories of father, from the viewpoint of a young teenager, I feel that to leave it there would do him less than justice. He was a kind man who was sensitive to the needs of others. Let me give you two examples. Father often took me with him on preaching missions to Leicestershire towns within cycling distance, such as Loughborough, Coalville, Ashby de la Zouch, Market Harborough and Melton Mowbray. In one of these towns we were always given a tea time meal by the same widowed sister. She lived on a small pension but enjoyed providing hospitality for preachers visiting from other assemblies. She invariably served them with a boiled egg along with brown bread and margarine.

On the visit I am writing about, I tapped off the top of my egg. The inside was black and the smell confirmed that it was obviously bad. I watched father with disbelief as he ate his egg which was just as bad as mine. As our host hobbled over to the fireplace to refill a pot of tea, he silently reached across the table and took my egg. Before returning the empty shell to the egg cup he had eaten my egg too! Our tea finished with chocolate cakes which she made from biscuit crumbs and cocoa powder.

During our cycle ride home I asked my father about the bad eggs and he said the same thing had happened to him on an earlier visit. Apparently the sister collected her eggs from the bottom of hedgerows around the neighbouring farm but father would not do or say anything that would upset or embarrass her. Father added that, upon reaching home, he would take an antidote, dill seeds, to prevent a stomach upset.

My father's other act of conspicuous kindness was to provide Granny Harwood with a home during the last few years of her life. Our maternal grandmother was visiting us when she was taken seriously ill. She was admitted to Leicester Royal Infirmary and was discharged within a few days. She had been diagnosed as terminally ill with stomach cancer. The hospital sent her home to die with the aid of the strongest drugs to help make her deep pain just bearable.

I will never forget the sight of father carrying granny into the house as tenderly as he would carry a small sick child. She was pale, helpless and dreadfully thin but after a few weeks of taking father's blood purifying mixtures she became a living testimony to the efficacy of his herbal remedies.

Granny Harwood lived well into her mid-seventies and for several years she helped mother with chores about the house. I recall, for instance, how she daily scrubbed and polished the front step of our house with a Cardinal wax polish. Not surprisingly our aged granny found her high-spirited grandchildren quite a trial. She said rather pensively one day, "You'll be sorry you said that after I've gone". Although we were only making fun of her quaint ways, we were nonetheless sorry to have been unkind to her. We knew, when she died, that Granny had at last gone to the Better Land that she often talked about. At her funeral my mother was crying and I had never seen that before.

For the very few outsiders who were permitted to visit the homes of Exclusive Brethren, it was like entering a time warp. The sad thing though is the Brethren's unshakeable belief that their cultural non-conformity is a necessary act of obedience to the teachings of the Bible, especially those in the letters of St. Paul. In reality their lifestyle and severe discipline is little more than the continuance of eighteenth century European rural life. The Amish and Mennonite people in the United States of America have based their lives on a similarly separatist interpretation of biblical rules and regulations. These are just my opinions but, while we may sympathetically admire the simple lifestyle of the Brethren, it must be said that if a strict system of laws replace the true freedom offered in the Christian message, this consigns its adherents to a life of bondage as a direct result of such cruel distortions of the truth.

# Chapter 14 - Army Service

When my National Service call-up papers came through the post, shortly before my eighteenth birthday, I followed my father's footsteps by registering as a conscientious objector. I appeared before a tribunal at Nottingham in November 1947. His Hon. Judge Norris and three members of the Tribunal heard my Application to be accepted as a conscientious objector to combatant service. I quote verbatim from the Tribunal's proceedings as these reveal my feelings or, at least, how I expressed them, in Brethren jargon, at the age of eighteen:

APPLICANT: I am a believer in the Lord Jesus Christ and am desirous that my movements be in accord with His holy will. In this respect I have a conscience against taking life. The general attitude and spirit of the Holy Scriptures relative to the present dispensation is one of grace, enhanced perfectly by the walk of the blessed Lord Jesus when here on earth, and representing God's attitude of grace and love toward mankind. Although hesitant in quoting a specific passage of Scripture the following words of the Lord to be found in the 18th chapter of John's Gospel verse 36, in my submission, supports this Application, "Jesus answered, my Kingdom is not of this world; and if my Kingdom was of this world, then would my servants fight, that I should not be delivered to the Jews: but now is my Kingdom not from hence."

FRIEND: I have known John from birth - he is a true and genuine Christian.

JUDGE: The Applicant is a Member of the Brethren. He objects only to Combatant Service. The Order of the Tribunal is that he should be registered as a person liable under National Service

(Armed Forces) to be called up for service but to be employed only in non-combatant duty.

Following the Tribunal's judgement I told the Ministry of Labour and National Service that I would like to serve the two years of National Service in the Army's NCC (Non Combatant Corps). The alternatives were to serve with a bomb disposal unit, the Royal Army Medical Corps or down a coalmine as a Bevin Boy. I passed the medical with an A1 grade and within a few weeks was instructed to report for service at the RPC (Royal Pioneer Corps) Depot in the NCC at Stourport-on-Severn in Worcestershire. A Travel Warrant to Kidderminster, the nearest railway station, was enclosed with the Enlistment Notice, together with, 'A Postal Order for 4 shillings in respect of an advance of service pay'.

I joined the Army at a time when garrisons for British troops were being disbanded all around the world. From 1947 and on through the 1950's, the British Empire was being replaced by the Commonwealth. Clement Atlee honoured his electoral pledge to grant independence to India, the Jewel of the Empire. In 1947 countries of the sub-continent became the first of many nations to break away from Britain on the friendliest of terms. Considering the manner in which Whitehall had behaved as masters of the Raj, this was a great achievement and was largely due to the political maturity of Jawaharlal Nehru and Mahatma Gandhi. Nehru, India's leader, was the Oxford educated intellectual and Gandhi the charismatic Father of the Nation. Britain left Palestine in 1948 and during the 1950's the disbandment of the Empire gathered pace with the independence of Kenya, Ghana, Nigeria and Jamaica.

On arrival at the barracks we were kitted out with standard Army uniform, a khaki battledress and a forage cap. We spent the first evening cleaning the webbing belt and gaiters with Blanco, brushing Dubbin into a pair of stiff leather boots, polishing our brass buttons, buckles and NCC cap badge with Duraglit. These were all minutely inspected when we appeared on parade the following morning.

I, for one, was intimidated by the RSM (Regimental Sergeant Major), with his barked commands and swagger stick. During our primary training he took us through some elementary parade ground drill in an attempt, against all odds, to knock us into some sort of military shape. During those six weeks of square-bashing the RSM stamped his soldierly discipline on us rookies. He called us in mock desperation, 'a shower', his term to describe the lowest of the low. I must say that he seemed to treat us 'wet behind the ears' recruits as objects worthy of his special contempt. It did not help either to see older NCC colleagues sniggering unsympathetically at our uncoordinated attempts at marching, changing step, about turns, marking time, saluting and other manoeuvres such as running at the double, standing to attention and standing at ease. The RSM gave the impression that his tough training methods had failed if any of his charges actually liked him.

The daily drill lasted about four hours and by that time every muscle ached. Then we had to spend the afternoons at the workplace assigned to us. The worst of these was, by common assent, the cookhouse duty. These jobs were sadistically assigned to recruits who came from privileged backgrounds, such as the occasional 'Hon.' and those who had been educated at public schools. One of the less savoury duties in the cookhouse was to chase cat-sized rats. Once the rodents were cornered, an RPC man, who was an expert executioner, swiftly despatched the exhausted rats with a hefty plank of wood.

In common with all Army recruits we were chased around and shouted at by boot-stamping NCO's (Non-Commissioned Officers) during the first few weeks. Early morning barrack room inspections were taken so seriously that some of us stayed awake all night because we were afraid of not getting our equipment and bedding all perfectly squared-up in time for the morning inspection. It was a tough discipline!

On the strength of my years' experience as a solicitor's articled clerk I was given a job in the Orderly Room, the general office at the RPC Depot. I was assigned to the daunting task of interviewing and taking statements from soldiers who were being held in detention prior to their trial by court martial. I knew little about Kings Regulations or the contents of the Manual of Military Law, which were necessary for the proper discharge of these duties. When I arrived in the Orderly Room I was presented with three Biro pens which were probably amongst the first Biros to be used in the British forces.

In addition to transcribing the interview I was responsible for summarising, for the benefit of the Defending Officer, the documentary evidence against the accused soldier.

I did my best to act, in the Army's terms, as a 'prisoner's friend'. The court consisted of three senior officers. After hearing the cases presented by the Prosecuting and Defending Officers, the court could sentence those it found guilty to a period of hard labour in the glasshouse (an army detention centre) or a dishonourable discharge from the Army. In more serious cases of treason or desertion during active service, a sentence of death by firing squad could be passed by the court. Although the other NCC recruits said I had the cushiest job of all, it was one that carried a heavy responsibility. I should mention that capital punishment was rare in peacetime and happily I never got involved in a case that carried such a serious sentence.

Pioneer Corps soldiers, who deserted during wartime, were still being picked up by Redcaps (the military police) and returned for trial to the RPC Depot at Stourport. By 1948 they were being arraigned on the lesser charge of being AWOL (Absent without Leave), which carried the maximum of a five year sentence in the glasshouse. One of those who I interviewed was still showing all the signs of being shell-shocked. This was the basis on which the court martial granted him a discharge from the Army on medical grounds.

I have to relate here an experience I had during my early weeks in the Army that deeply disturbed me. Because of my special duties in the Orderly Room I was billeted in a hut with an NCO. After a time I was awakened in the middle of the night by the NCO trying to get into bed with me. I was shocked because I instinctively knew that his intentions were not honourable. I fended off his advances and reported the incident the next day to the camp Adjutant. Thankfully, I never saw the NCO again and hope that other recruits were spared from a similarly traumatic experience. I sadly suffered a loss of innocence and the memory of it is still an unpleasant one.

After that night I slept in a communal hut with the other NCC's in my section. The most trying part of army life, for me, was the strident sound of the regimental bugler who blew reveille every morning at 06.00 hours. On the positive side, I came to enjoy parading in army uniform. This consisted of: a well creased khaki battledress and trousers, a highly polished pair of boots from which the expression 'spit and polish' was derived, a belt, a pair of spats that were treated daily to a fresh dose of Blanco and the forage cap, with its well-polished brass NCC badge.

Most of my NCC comrades came from Brethren homes so we attended the weekly meetings at the Assembly in Stourport. It was a twenty minute walk across the fields from our barracks. The few families in the Assembly were extremely hospitable, generously providing us with meals. The two dairy farmers in the meeting supplied the others with supplies of meat, milk, butter and eggs.

We often shopped in the nearby town of Kidderminster so that we could provide our hosts with fruit and vegetables. As we were only paid twenty-eight shillings a week our spending power, after nightly visits to the NAAFI (Navy, Army and Air Force Institute), was rather limited. This was a good example of how beneficial it was to have the security of belonging to the Brethren. It seemed that in every place to which we could be posted, in the UK as well as Malta, Hong Kong and Germany, there were always homes that provided members with warm Christian fellowship.

Despite the outward display of religious conformity I became quite a rebel whilst serving in the Army. As a result, I was criticised by my more pious fellows for playing football on Saturday afternoons rather than travelling to some distant fellowship meeting. In their judgement I was getting my priorities wrong by involving myself in worldly activities. No doubt some of them felt vindicated when, during one match, I was carried off the field and taken to the military hospital in Worcester.

An x-ray showed that I had sustained a badly fractured ankle during a particularly tough tackle. My foot and leg were encased in plaster and I was admitted to the hospital's orthopaedic ward. Within a few days I was allowed out. With the aid of crutches and the red, white and blue uniform, I went to watch a cricket match in which Worcestershire played the Australian touring side. The Worcestershire County Cricket ground is an idyllic setting surrounded, as it is, by Worcester Cathedral and the River Severn. I had never been happier, not least because Don Bradman played one of his last first class innings in Worcester, just a few weeks before his final test appearance in England.

Some of my NCC friends visited me in hospital and envied me the cushy life of good food, pretty nurses and comfortable beds. But, it must be admitted, I derived even greater pleasure from the visits of Royal Pioneer Corps soldiers. They not only paid their own travelling expenses but sacrificed their Saturday or Sunday morning lie in to come to Worcester. During their visits I was able to help them in ways they much appreciated back at the barracks. They did not have the advantage of being able to read and write so we found a quiet spot in the hospital grounds where I could read to them individually a letter they had received and write a reply as they dictated it.

On my first contact with these regular soldiers I was put off by some of their less attractive behaviour, such as drunken brawls on Saturday nights, bad language and bragging about promiscuity. However, after joining in their sports and writing letters for them, we became really good friends. They were also respectfully quiet when I knelt to pray before getting into bed at night. Some wanted to talk about their personal family circumstances and a few admitted to a feeling of purposeless in life. I knew that the Brethren meetings would be too cerebral for them so, in addition to giving them various tracts and telling them how God had helped me discover the meaning of life, I suggested that they attend the regular services conducted by the Camp Padre.

Incidentally, a month after my demobilisation I was amused to receive an impressive looking silver medal in recognition of the injury I got playing football. It was called The King's Badge. The head of King George VI was on one side and the reverse was inscribed, "AWARDED FOR VALOUR to Pte. John Fear of the NCC". The letter that accompanied it said, "The Minister of Pensions is commanded by His Majesty the King to forward to you the King's Badge for members of the Armed Forces who are disabled as a result of war service".

I said earlier that I was something of a rebel in the NCC. Unlikely as it may sound, I was twice charged with the serious offence of 'maliciously damaging government property'. Let me tell you about the incidents that brought me before the Commanding Officer.

To give me the necessary privacy for reading and writing the men's letters, the sergeant thoughtfully arranged for me to have the sole occupancy of a small nissen hut. During the bitterly cold winter months of 1948 I used, in defiance of army regulations, a portable single-bar electric fire. The snow storms were so heavy that farmers had to walk over the top of hedges and through snow drifts that almost touched the telegraph wires to rescue flocks of sheep and cattle that lay buried after the blizzards. Early one morning I left the hut, during a power cut that had blacked out the whole camp, but neglected to take the precaution of disconnecting the fire from its socket. When the electrical supply was restored the fire was knocked over, perhaps by one of the many cats or rodents that roamed the barracks in search of food. In any event the lighted fire started a blaze that destroyed the hut and its contents.

As I was standing in line on pay parade, the sound of fire engines rang out across the parade ground. I later learned, with horror, that the firemen were on their way to fighting my blazing hut. Soon after the fire our Adjutant ordered that I should be placed under house arrest. I now faced the indignity of appearing before a court martial, which was a most unusual experience for a soldier in the ranks of the NCC. On the morning of the hearing one of the two military escorts took away my cap, belt and bootlaces. After I had been quick-stepped into the court the Presiding Officer accepted my plea of not guilty to the charge of 'maliciously damaging government property'. The Colonel asked why I had done it. I remember standing rigidly to attention and saying, "It was an accident, Sir". There was a long pause while he consulted other members of the court. I was relieved when he reprimanded me for carelessness and only gave me the relatively light sentence of 30 days Confined to Barracks, with no financial penalty. I was marched out and that was the end of the main ordeal.

The second incident that got me into trouble with the authorities came when I went to a day long course at a rundown Army camp near Oxford. The course was conducted by officials from the War Department and the subject was 'Administrative Procedures in the Armed Services'. It was a welcome day out and after a good buffet lunch some of us explored sections of the barracks that consisted entirely of derelict huts. We found the most satisfying way of letting off steam was to hurl stones at those pieces of glass that still hung from the hut's window frames. I was so preoccupied with the stone throwing that I failed to notice the sudden approach of a couple of the camp's military police. It was ridiculous, but typical of the Army, that I should be charged with breaking scores of windows i.e. the total number of windows originally fitted to the hut. I spoke up at the hearing and said the whole thing was a nonsense. The

Commanding Officer must have agreed with me because all I got was a reprimand.

Many of the men who had been enlisted for National Service felt that the period spent in uniform was a complete waste of time. Some of these men showed their frustration and impatience by keeping, on the wall of the barracks behind their bed, a countdown chart on which they noted the remaining months, weeks and days before their estimated date of demobilisation (demob day).

From the very beginning of my army service I felt that I could usefully spend the two years in a training programme that would be a helpful preparation for my future civilian career. This led me to enrol in a correspondence course offered by a London college that specialised in this sort of education. The college claimed that their courses were equivalent to a London University external Bachelor of Arts Degree course. The Army heavily subsidised the course fees but unlike the present Open University courses there were no personal tutorials, television programmes or radio broadcasts to supplement the written syllabus. It was a struggle to keep up with the intensive course of study but after eighteen months I took three examinations, together with two other students, under the supervision of members of the Adjutant's staff. My efforts were rewarded with three good passes in Economics, English Language and Elementary Politics.

After serving over a year of my National Service at the Royal Pioneer Corps Depot at Stourport, I was posted to the northern headquarters of the RPC based in Yorkshire. My train from Worcester was met at the York railway station by the driver of an army jeep who took me to Sandhutton Hall (a stately home that had been requisitioned by the War Office). It is several miles from York.

I instantly fell in love with Sandhutton Hall with its air of gracious living: wood panelled rooms, stained glass windows, huge tiled kitchens and the picturesque lake that was only a stone's throw from the rear terrace.

It was there that I was introduced to freshwater fishing and after a few days of trying to catch a fish with a borrowed rod I caught a huge and fierce looking pike. After landing the fish I got the impression that the toothy pike was chasing me. After a heart-stopping moment one of my fellow fishermen managed to release the pike from its hook and returned it to the lake.

Once again my duties included the preparation of the defence for those who were held waiting trial by court martial. I was given the honorary rank of Sergeant so that I had the necessary seniority to carry out this work. Courts martial law is a combination of the adversarial and the inquisitorial systems of justice. The first is practised in the civil courts of Britain, where both the prosecuting and defending advocates do their best to secure the fairest result that serves the cause of justice. The alternative system is devoted to a search for truth in the interest of all parties concerned in the case. In a court martial the defending officer is responsible for collecting and presenting the strongest evidence for the defence of the accused. The 'search for truth', by the direct questioning of the accused and witnesses, is the prime responsibility of the presiding officer.

The nearest Brethren Assembly was in Leeds, according to my Directory of Assemblies. On my first off duty Sunday I cycled, on an army despatch riders' bike, to York, for the 20 minute train journey from York to Leeds. I duly presented my Letter of Commendation from the Saints Assembling in Leicester. When it was read out at the beginning of the Morning Meeting I hardly recognised myself because of the fulsome phrases used to describe me. As I was the first NCC soldier they had seen I was something of a novelty. There was some competition as to who would offer me hospitality, i.e. take me home for lunch. Eventually I spent the whole day with a widow and her two teenage daughters. Predictably I was swept off my feet, romantically, by the younger of the girls. This led to me getting into trouble with the civil police.

I arrived back on the last train from Leeds after spending the evening with her. It was about midnight when I unchained the borrowed army bike at York station. The cycle did not carry any lights but it did have a mailbag carrier fitted to the front. Just as I was about to cycle off, an RPC soldier, who had arrived on the same train, persuaded me to give him a lift on the carrier. As I remember it we weaved uncertainly around a corner on the outskirts of York, straight into the arms of a police sergeant. Several weeks later I was summoned to appear in the local Magistrates' Court. The Magistrates duly fined me £2 for 'carrying two passengers on a bicycle that was only constructed for one' and £1 for 'failing to display lights during the hours of darkness'. This episode turned me into one of the lads, in the eyes of the regular soldiers at Sandhutton Hall. Several of them came forward to contribute towards the fines, which represented almost three weeks' pay.

There was very little to do in camp, especially when the week's pay had run out, so the men's main enemy was boredom. A nucleus of twenty men in my hut responded to the suggestion that we should organise a debate once a week. They liked this because, as much as anything, it provided an alternative to their endless card games and involved those that were not all that literate. We drew up a list of subjects for debate and there seemed to be no limit to the topics that the soldiers nominated for discussion. The most popular were connected with ethics, religion, relationships and politics. The Padre, who joined us occasionally, got permission for us to use a spare room in the Hall. These debating sessions sometimes ended abruptly, without a vote, when there was only sufficient time left to order a last pint in the NAAFI before closing time. I came to realise that I was really privileged to live with and get to know these fine men. They all became much more articulate as a result of participating in the debates.

During my time at the Hall I also spent some of my free time open air preaching in the surrounding Yorkshire countryside. It must have seemed an unusual sight, for the villagers, to see a young soldier preaching all alone on their village green! Occasionally I was accompanied by RPC mates who tagged along as a sort of unofficial bodyguard.

One of the perks available to National Servicemen was the provision of three railway vouchers a year. These entitled the holder to a return journey from the nearest station to their base to any destination in the UK. The intention of the authorities was to get the recruit home but I took advantage of the provision to travel further afield. On a couple of my longer leave periods I travelled as far north and as far south as the rail network then allowed. During the week I journeyed north I explored the Scottish cities of Glasgow, Edinburgh, Inverness and Aberdeen. I also spent a night at the east coast port of Petershead where most of the fishermen were members of the local Exclusive Brethren assembly. On a subsequent occasion I applied for a voucher from York to the Isle of Wight. I spent a couple of memorable nights, en route, at the Union Jack Club, a Victorian building across the road from Waterloo Station in London. The Club (which no longer exists) was a noisy, down at heel hostel for serving members of the Armed Forces who were on leave in London. Accommodation at five shillings a night was in rows of wooden cubicles. A breakfast of sausage, mashed potato and baked beans was included in the price.

During those two days I marvelled at the capital's main historic attractions. On reaching the Isle of Wight I was too hungry to take in the Island's beauties, having spent my last few coppers for a cup of tea and sandwich on the ferry from Portsmouth. I therefore beat a hasty retreat to the mainland and made my way to Leicester where I knew that I could get a good hearty meal at my parents' ever welcoming table.

It is unusual to admit to enjoying National Service but for me it was a formative experience. It gave me space to breath and develop as an individual. Adversity can strengthen one's Christian convictions and this was certainly my experience. As I look back on those two years in the Army I feel equal gratitude to those Brethren families who gave me such generous hospitality and to my RPC friends who allowed me to help them in various practical ways.

# Chapter 15 - Civvy Street

All I had to show materially for the two years of National Service was a badly fitting demob suit and discharge papers, which rather surprisingly, described my term of service as 'exemplary'. The Royal Pioneer Corps Major, who signed my Soldier's Release Book said, "Private Fear, J. (NCC) has been employed at this HQ as Orderly Room Clerk. He is most intelligent and a very willing worker. I have always found him honest, sober, clean, reliable and trustworthy."

Just before I came home, Granny Harwood had died at the age of 77. Granny was never the little old lady, in a shawl, feebly crocheting in the chimney corner. She played an energetic part in our home life right to the end. She really seemed to enjoy black leading the fire grate and adding a daily coat of red polish to the pavement front step. She was a tireless and faithful servant of God and an inspiration to all who came under her influence. She radiated the joy of living and of giving.

When I visited the office of the solicitor, to whom I had been articled during the year prior to my army service, I was shocked to discover that he had died a few weeks earlier. This upset all my plans because I fully expected to resume my law training with him. As the articles were free, I had little realistic prospect of finding another principal who would take me on as a pupil under such privileged terms. After several week's demob leave I signed on at the local Employment Exchange. The dole (unemployment pay) was means-tested and after considerable form filling I was given the standard single man's allowance of fifteen shillings (75 pence) a week. The official at the Exchange thought that, in view of my examination success and clerical experience in the Army, I should be able to get a temporary non-established job in the Civil Service.

After an interview with the local Income Tax Inspector I was offered a post that was described as Clerical Assistant.

As the Civil Service post was not available for at least a month, Paul (my younger brother) and I began to make plans for a holiday together in France. Paul had recently left Grammar School where he had picked up a good set of grades in his matriculation examination. We had often talked of going to France for a hitchhiking holiday and, on the strength of the confidence I had gained in the Army and Paul's ability to speak the French language, we talked our parents into letting us travel to Paris.

We took the channel ferry from Dover to Dunkirk. As it was vacation time, in August 1951, we were fortunately able to rent a couple of student rooms, for a fortnight. Our rooms were in the College Franco-Brittanique which is on the campus of the Cité Universitaire. Paris lived up to all my expectations. I loved everything about France - the people, the art, the food and drink, chaotic traffic, the exquisite smells of freshly baked bread and the aroma of roasted coffee. We spent hours gazing into the colourful shop windows and made frequent cheap journeys on the Metro (underground) trains.

Just to be overseas, handling French money and hearing the excitable French language spoken was all so memorable. During our first few days we walked the length and breadth of the bustling Champs-Élysées, gazing into the window of a tempting Parisian patisserie, before ending up under the Arc de Triomphe. The eternal flame at the memorial to the Unknown Soldier was constantly guarded by a group of French troops. I stood and wondered why the flame never went out.

Although living on a limited budget we picnicked in style on the banks of the River Seine. Most days we lunched on baguettes, still warm from the oven, cheese and cheap local wine. We also bought fruit from street markets where stall holders were happy for us to select from heaps of peaches, nectarines, melons and apricots. Our al fresco lunches left us in a relaxed mood for exploring the most famous of the French capital's museums, churches and monuments. We were breathless at the end of the climb to the top of the Eiffel Tower but the view was worth the effort. We were also impressed by Napoleon's Tomb, with its classical design and cool, polished marble. However, when we finally came face to face with the world's most enigmatic lady, the Mona Lisa, situated in the Louvre, I was disappointed. It was such a small, drab painting.

I never got used to visiting gents' toilets in Paris. There were two basic types and both left me feeling embarrassed. The outdoor variety was constructed of a three-sided metal box that only concealed the middle third of the user's body. When I was forced to use these facilities I was quite convinced that passers-by on the pavement were looking at my head, shoulders and legs as these were clearly visible through the grilled areas at the top and bottom of the six foot high screens. I was quite shaken when I first entered the row of cubicles that were provided in railway stations and at the rear of larger restaurants. I fled in panic because I thought I must have made a mistake when I encountered a formidable looking woman, in a white coat, who was sitting inside the entrance handing out rolls of toilet paper. However, when I checked the outside of the door, it was clearly profiled with a male figure.

As I returned my roll of toilet paper, the attendant hissed at me as I had neglected to add to the pile of coins in the dish on the table in front of her. Although this was an unintentional lapse it was probably the most appropriate response to the disgusting facilities provided in her establishment. Within a few days we located a city centre hotel. Their well-appointed gents' cloakroom could be easily entered without attracting the attention of staff on duty at the hotel's reception desk. The cloakroom was pure luxury with hot and cold running water, clean towels, clothes brushes, French cologne and after-shave lotion. The glass-fronted cisterns, even in the cubicles, had goldfish swimming around in the water!

Paul was an ideal travelling companion, not least because we both shared the same cultural interests in France. We usually ended the day with a visit to the University's canteen where generous portions of 'oeufs aux mayonnaise' were served until midnight. We talked long into the night about things that had happened whilst I had been in the Army. Perhaps the saddest of these was the serious rift that had developed between Paul and our father.

My brother said that father let no opportunity pass without asserting his rather heavy handed authority. I sympathised with both of them. Paul had become quite a hero in the eyes of his younger brothers and sisters, not only because of his educational achievements but for his impressive physique. Father probably felt that his own authority was being undermined by these attributes, not least because he had sacrificed so much to get Paul through his Grammar School years. With two such strong minded individuals a final showdown was inevitable. The fateful clash came shortly after we returned home from France.

I still do not know what caused it but was sickened to witness the undignified struggle that raged between the two of them in a dark passage between our living room and kitchen. Apparently Paul had grabbed the cane after father had aimed a vicious swish of it in his direction. Father was incoherent with rage as they grappled for possession of the cane. Paul was the first to disengage from this embarrassing encounter. With a voice that trembled with passion father ordered Paul to his bedroom. When I went to bed hours later Paul was already asleep.

Quite understandably Paul had by now had enough of father, whom he saw as a tyrant. Early next morning we were startled to discover a note from my brother saying that he had decided to run away from home. I do not know how my father did it but by mid-morning he had tracked Paul down to the Army Recruitment office in the centre of Leicester. Perhaps the Brethren network had been at work, having been alerted to Paul's absence from home. All this, however, was to no avail. Father tried to persuade the Army recruitment officer to let him take Paul home. The officer refused because Paul (who was 18) was old enough to join the Army and in addition he had paid the contractual King's Shilling.

From such an unpromising start, Paul's army career went rather well. I think he originally signed on for fifteen years but after quite a short time he entered the Royal Military Academy at Sandhurst where he trained as an Officer Cadet. His contemporaries included the Duke of Kent and King Hussein of Jordan. (Paul has only recently retired from the Army with the rank of Colonel. He married a German nursing sister, Gundola, and they have two daughters.)

# Chapter 16 - Civil Service

It took us children several months to come to terms with Paul's sudden and sad departure from home. It was a stunning blow to all of us! I was perhaps the one who missed him most, because Paul and I had happily assumed a paternalistic role in the lives of our four younger siblings.

On one occasion, during a period of leave from the Army, all six of us conspired together to visit Jerome's Photographic Studio in the centre of Leicester. It was great fun but I do not know how we managed to do it without our parents' knowledge. Our plans to have the photograph taken secretly needed to be quite elaborate because Mary was only three years old at the time. We allowed two hours for the tram journeys to and from town and time to keep the thirty minute appointment at the studio as well. The resultant photograph shows us standing in a well arranged group, primly dressed in our Sunday best clothes and looking suitably conspiratorial.

When we finally presented mother and father with the photograph, they seemed genuinely puzzled as to how we had managed to get it taken without their knowledge. They were, however, pleased with the result. On another leave I took David and Elizabeth for a day trip to London where we saw some of the capital's best known tourist attractions. A street photographer took a photo of the three of us in Trafalgar Square. In it I look proud to be wearing army uniform, with my forage cap at a jaunty angle.

Shortly after Paul left home I took up the clerical post that I had been offered at the local Tax Inspector's office. It did not take long for me to realise that, as a temporary Tax Officer, I was at the bottom of the administrative ladder.

About this time I developed a number of physical symptoms, which my doctor felt needed a series of clinical investigations. He referred me to an outpatient clinic at Leicester's City General Hospital. The early symptoms were a sudden loss of weight, a tremor in my hands and a faster than normal pulse rate. Shortly afterwards my eyes grew more prominent and my neck was becoming noticeably thicker. The hospital consultant said these were classic signs of an overactive thyroid gland and a condition known as thyrotoxicosis.

The specialist enquired whether I had experienced some recent psychological disturbance or if there had been some trauma in the family. Apparently such shocks are known to trigger off a malfunction in the thyroid gland. We came to the conclusion that the symptoms first appeared around the time that Paul left home. This upset could have led, in part, to the onset of my illness. The thyroid gland's main function is to regulate the rate of the body's metabolism. One of the hospital doctors explained that an overactive thyroid gland acted on the heart in much the same way as a car engine would if the driver kept his foot permanently on the vehicle's accelerator.

At the conclusion of the appropriate tests the specialist recommended the least radical of the three alternative treatments available at the time. He was against surgery or injections of radioactive iodine because these were irreversible procedures. Instead he prescribed a course of drug therapy that was designed to neutralise the chemical imbalance which caused the hyperactivity of the thyroid. Thankfully these drugs arrested and stabilised the growth of the debilitating aspects of the disease. During the several years I was taking the drugs, I had weekly blood tests at the hospital.

Meanwhile, I slipped back into the life of our local Brethren Assembly as though I had never been away. I now quite enjoyed the meetings and took a regular part in them. I also caught up on the many books of ministry that had been published whilst I had been away in the Army. Perhaps the elders noted my renewed interest because they asked me to take on a couple of new responsibilities. Some interpreted this as an apprenticeship for a leadership role in the future.

One of my responsibilities was to read, to the assembled Brethren, the chapter selected for each Sunday afternoon's Bible Reading. The other responsibility was to count and bank the proceeds of the weekly collection. This was taken up as an integral part of the weekly Breaking of Bread service. I was also invited to preach at an occasional Sunday evening Gospel Meeting. These 'promotions' provoked some hostility towards me on the part of parents whose sons of my age group were not given a similar accolade. This, at least, was how it seemed to me.

I was also keen to gain promotion from my lowly position in the Civil Service. The opportunity came when I was nominated, by my immediate superior, for an Open Competitive Examination. This selected graduates for the executive ranks of the established Civil Service and was a two day examination held in London. The main written papers were designed to test the candidate's general intelligence and knowledge of basic academic subjects. Others were aimed at testing their ability to analyse data and solve problems. The oral parts of the examination tested our ability to work well as a member of a team and to evaluate our communication skills. The final written questionnaire was designed to reveal any signs of psychological instability.

As this was an Open Competitive Examination, I had hoped to be awarded a high enough place to gain entry to the Foreign Office and its diplomatic service. However, the examiners placed my name in the middle range of successful candidates. I was offered a post as an Immigration or Customs & Excise Officer, both located in one of the channel ports. The other post on offer was to take a more senior, established position in the local tax office. In normal circumstances I would have preferred one of the former jobs but with my health problems and new responsibilities in the Brethren Assembly, I elected to stay at home in Leicester.

Before the appointment could be confirmed I was required to sign the Official Secrets Act. There was also a medical examination to ensure that I qualified for the Civil Service pension scheme. As a result of my examination success I became a Tax Officer (Higher Grade). Although the public perceive tax officials as heartless zealots, who devote their time in the pursuit of fraudsters and tax evaders, I was glad to discover that the majority of my colleagues tried to be helpful to individual taxpayers. Our primary role was to advise taxpayers how to prepare a detailed account of what they earned and how much tax they had paid, so that they could claim additional allowances or apply for any refund to which they were entitled. Of course, if these enquiries uncovered fraud or tax evasion, then these would be dealt with according to the regulations.

To be honest I was not sufficiently numerate to feel comfortable with the job. For instance, this was the period before pocket calculators were in use and one of the most common tax allowances involved a fraction of 2/9th's. I was only a plodder at the best of times which meant that my workload was constantly in arrears. I would have left and found another job but as important changes were taking place in our family circumstances, it did not seem the right time to give up the security and good salary that the Civil Service provided.

# PART 4 - MARRIAGE AND MINISTRY

John and Mary

# Chapter 17 - Meeting Mary

Having secured a permanent appointment in the British Civil Service, my thoughts turned to marriage. The prize of a well-paid job and a good pension at the end of it, in 40 years' time, turned out to be something of an anti-climax.

In my new grade I no longer had the job satisfaction of dealing with individual taxpayers who came to the counter. I had previously enjoyed helping visitors complete their annual return forms and giving them advice on how to claim the maximum tax allowances to which their circumstances entitled them. My experience is that while the tax man is keen to trap the dodgers, he is equally willing to show the honest way through the statutory maze.

I was now under constant pressure to conform to performance targets and this was not easy because I possessed little natural aptitude for the complex figures involved. Added to this, was the need to resist the pressure put on me to join the recognised trade union, the Inland Revenue Staff Federation. This arose both through my personal conviction about the inequities of the closed shop, as well as the need to conform to Brethren prohibitions against trade union membership.

Despite these problems I must have had good relations with the staff because my departmental colleagues arranged a surprise birthday tea to commemorate my 21st birthday. The cake was decorated, much to my embarrassment, with a large silver horseshoe. This remained hidden in my desk drawer until the day I finally left the Tax Office.

This then was the background that led me to actively embark on the road to matrimony. Such a move marked a significant turning point for children of Exclusive Brethren parents since broken engagements rarely happened and divorce was unknown. The field for prospective marriage partners was strictly limited. Just as a Jew regarded the marriage of one of their own to a non-Jew as 'dead', so the Exclusive Brethren treated one of their children who married a non-member, as though the new couple ceased to exist.

The pressure to find a wife came as much from my hormones as to the need to conform to the Brethren tradition of sons marrying in their late teens or early twenties. By tradition we relied heavily on the facilities provided by the Saturday afternoon Fellowship Meetings as an opportunity to meet a suitable life partner. These were also known as Tea Meetings because sandwiches, cakes and a cup of tea were served between the two hour long meetings. There was a constant tinkling of china as the cups and saucers, placed under each seat, were disturbed by children and others moving around the Meeting Room. The serving of the tea meal was carried out by single brothers and sisters who used the opportunity to hold tentative conversations with potential suitors.

If these regular regional meetings had not existed it would have been necessary to invent them. This is because these gatherings also provided the cement that kept the structure of the Exclusive Brethren in a good functioning state of repair. Later on I came to believe that the Fellowship Meetings exercised a sinister control over the membership of the hundreds of affiliated assemblies worldwide. At this stage, however, I was happy to make use of their proven matchmaking potential. During the meetings there were many references to the fact that we were 'walking in the light'. This left me wondering about other Christians who were, by inference, 'walking in darkness'. If any question was raised, however, we were told that each person would be judged by God according to the measure of light they had received.

Meetings were arranged on a regional basis and for those of us living in the East Midlands the two main venues were Nottingham and Leicester. These alternated every other week with less frequent meetings taking place in Derby, Loughborough, Northampton and Peterborough. I did, as it happened, like a young sister in Leicester. However, she was not only a couple of years my senior but her parents were also looking out for a better prospect. On their behalf, her quartet of brothers made sure that I was kept at arm's length. Apart from her there was nobody else in the region to whom I felt really attracted in terms of a long-term, loving relationship.

The neighbouring circuit of Fellowship Meetings were held in the West Midlands and these were based in Birmingham and Coventry with subsidiary meetings taking place in Leamington, Stratford-upon-Avon and Kenilworth. The elders in Leicester must have sensed my frustration because one of them drew me to one side and gave me details of the next Fellowship Meeting in Kenilworth. With the encouragement of my parents I set out for Coventry on a Midland Red double-decker bus. Coventry's main bus station was the only area left intact after the bombing blitz on the city centre in 1944. Nearby a new Cathedral was rising up from the bombed out remains of the old building.

The bus journey to Kenilworth took about twenty minutes. I travelled on the top deck and shortly after we had passed the Kenilworth sign I saw a striking looking girl standing on the pavement, apparently waiting to cross the road.

There was something about her that had me acting quite irrationally. I rushed downstairs just in time to jump off the back platform before the bus proceeded on its journey to the town centre. I quickly ran back to where I had seen the girl standing and, much to my relief, she was still there. She was wearing a smart school uniform and apart from her well-groomed, flaxen haired plaits, I was helplessly smitten by the shy smile that lit up her friendly face.

I realised that a clumsy approach could have frightened her away so I just asked her if she could help me find the road in which the Kenilworth Meeting Room was located. I remember being so relieved when, instead of rejecting me, she offered to show me the road as she was going that way as well.

Within a few minutes I discovered that she was a 'sister' on her way to the Fellowship Meeting. As I sat next to her in the hall waiting for the first Bible Reading, I reflected that as someone who had been brought up to commit everything of consequence to God in prayer I had begun the journey to Kenilworth by asking for God's help in finding a wife. As I sat in the hushed atmosphere I dared to hope that God's answer to my prayer was sitting alongside me.

As the customary cups of tea, sandwiches and cakes were served during the tea interval I got to know as much about her as seemed polite. Her name was Mary Grace, she was 17 and a pupil in her final year at Warwick High School for Girls. Mary was an only child and lived with her parents in Kenilworth. Mary's father, Ralph, was an optician and pharmacist. I had already heard of him because he held a fairly senior rank among the leading Brethren speakers in the West Midlands. Her mother, Olive, was a 'Martha type' and one of her anxieties concerned the possibility of her only daughter being left on the shelf.

When she introduced me to her parents, Mary's mother welcomed me with open arms while her father was gracious but distinctly reserved. He had hoped that Mary was about to embark on a five year optical course in Birmingham. In retrospect my sympathies are entirely on his side because I must have seemed to him an untimely and unpromising prospect for the hand of his beloved daughter. Mary was a star pupil at King's High School, Warwick and in July 1950 gained three distinctions and five credits at her matriculation examination.

For my part I had never before believed in the romantic sentiment of 'love at first sight' but this time there was no doubting the reality of it. This initial and unforgettable encounter with Mary left me rather breathless and with my head in the clouds, as I journeyed back to Leicester.

# Chapter 18 - Courtship

After this promising start, Mary became the obsessive object of my romantic attentions. I thought about her incessantly and for several weeks we wrote regular letters to each other. To be honest, I do not think Mary was particularly impressed by me but I pursued her quite relentlessly. It paid off because Mary's mother eventually invited me to spend a weekend in Kenilworth.

My relationship with Mrs. Lynes was always rather strained and beginning with this first visit, she tried to persuade me to accept the plans she had mapped out for her daughter's future. Mary was an only child because following her birth a major gynaecological operation was necessary and this prevented Mary's mother from bearing further children. This loss brought great sadness to her life. She looked to me, I think, to restore her sense of self-worth. I was, however, insufficiently emotionally mature to let her have her way on all the issues that arose between us.

Rather unexpectedly, Mary's father and I developed a relaxed relationship and a mutual respect for each other. I was immensely flattered by the whole-hearted interest he took in my Civil Service prospects. I was impressed too by the way he encouraged me in the various Brethren activities in which I was involved. He could so easily have crushed the root of self-confidence that had been slowly nurturing during my time in the Army and as a result of my recent examination successes. Not that he was blind to my temperamental flaws, the tendency to exaggerate for example. He knew how to gently prick such signs of pomposity. I like to think that he took me in hand in the role of a surrogate son.

Several weeks after my first weekend in Kenilworth, Mary paid a reciprocal visit to our home in Leicester. I was acutely aware of the social gulf that existed between our two families but unlike the established Church of England, the Brethren was quite a classless movement. The early Victorian founders of the Brethren were Irish landed clergy and members of the English aristocracy. In their large houses, masters and servants worshipped together at the beginning of each working day and in formal Sunday Services. During subsequent generations, marriages took place between the upper and lower classes. In due time the resulting progeny represented the widest spectrum of contemporary society. I was probably quite a snob because I aspired to the middle class of which Mary was a member rather than to the lower class to which my parents belonged.

When Mary finally arrived at our modest home she adapted perfectly and genuinely enjoyed the lifestyle of my four brothers and sisters. Everyone welcomed her into our home and I was as proud as a peacock sitting next to her during our Sunday meetings, not least because Mary's father was held in high esteem by the elders in our local Assembly.

Strange as it may seem, I was disappointed with Mary's first visit to our home. From the moment of her arrival she was taken over by the entire Fear clan and their many mealtime guests. She revelled in the experience of sharing a bedroom with my two sisters. Obviously I was too possessive because I was expecting to have as much of Mary to myself as I did in Kenilworth. I suppose we were a typical courting couple, enjoying long walks and intimate talks together.

About a year after we first met Mary agreed to my proposal that we should get engaged, provided I could obtain her father's approval. I normally found Mr. Lynes quite approachable but on this occasion I was incredibly tense. I suspect he knew the direction our talk was taking us when I related to him the story of Isaac and Rebekah in the 24th chapter of Genesis. He let me stumble through my ordeal without trying to interrupt me. I pointed out that Isaac signified his commitment to Rebekah by presenting her with a ring. I concluded my well-rehearsed petition by asking him whether, in view of this Biblical precedent, he would permit me to become betrothed (another good Biblical word) to his daughter. This provoked his dry sense of humour because without a pause he said, "Of course, you will have realised, John, that it would have been a nose-ring". With a twinkle in his eye he quickly added that an engagement would have his blessing.

The following Saturday found Mary and I gazing in the window of a Coventry jeweller's shop. Mary finally selected a ring with a price-tag of £24. It was a gold ring with three matching diamonds. After the necessary size adjustment and visit to the bank, I collected the ring. We were formally engaged, in Kenilworth, during the following weekend.

Right up to the eve of our marriage Mary's mother threatened to call off our engagement and return the wedding presents. The possibility of her daughter remaining on the shelf, however, proved to be quite a deterrent in the end.

In the early 1950's Britain was at the peak of its post-war house building programme. Local authorities were funding the building of council houses which replaced the prefab estates that were temporarily erected on bombed sites at the end of the war. The government also subsidised the private market by giving generous allowances against the payment of interest on Building Society mortgages. With 90 per cent loans available at 4 per cent interest it was a favourable time for us to enter the private housing market.

Mary and I quickly agreed on the area in Leicester where we wanted to set up our first home together. I had always regarded Knighton as a posh suburb of the city. It was situated midway between the last stop on the Leicester Corporation bus route and the beginning of the green belt that served as a buffer area between the city's southern boundary and the rural villages of Leicestershire. A well-known local builder had just started a new development close to the green belt, so we selected a corner plot of land that had already been marked out for a semi-detached, three bedroom house.

Our grass verged road led to a nearby meadow and the house agent assured us that the builder would be advertising for an ironmonger, grocer, fishmonger and a shoe repairer to open a parade of shops on the estate. All the new houses were mock Tudor, half stuccoed semis, but they represented Shangri-La for buyers who wanted to climb onto the lower rungs of the management ladder. At least we had small gardens, fresh air, new schools and an efficient bus service to take the bread winners to their jobs in banks, offices, shops and local services.

Now that we had selected a house, our timetable was determined by the progress of its construction. We agreed a date for the exchange of contracts so that it would coincide with the date when I could save the 15 per cent (£300) deposit we were due to pay towards the basic purchase price of £1,950. Mary's parents agreed that we should get married on 28th August 1954, just a month following the house's completion date.

I cycled to Knighton at least twice a week to check on the progress of our house. When the foundations had been laid it seemed far too small for the two living rooms, entrance hall and kitchen that had been shown on the builder's plan. As the building progressed this fear proved to be unfounded. I was so excited by this new venture that I even regularly cut the grass verges that separated the two pavements and the roads on which the plot stood.

Although the houses on the new development were virtually identical, we spent happy hours selecting the colours in which the inside and outside of the house would be painted. We were also given the option of choosing two fireplaces from a range of six designs. That took an afternoon at the showroom of the local builders' merchant. We agreed to spend the barest minimum on extras. In fact, all we spent above the basic price was £12 for a two-door serving hatch between the kitchen and the drawing room. We called our home 'Kenilworth' and took possession of the keys, as well as signing the conveyancing documents, just two weeks before the date of our marriage.

It was my strong nest-building instinct that caused a temporary breach between Mary's parents and myself. I suppose, in common with other betrothed couples, we had a series of ups and downs. Perhaps our most serious down arose over the financial contribution Mr. and Mrs. Lynes wanted to make towards our future home. Call it ego, pride or the desire for independence - I possessed them all in full measure. I did not come out of this clash with much credit but it seemed perfectly reasonable to me at the time that I should be left with the responsibility for the care of my future wife.

Mary could not understand what all the fuss was about but after the initial skirmishes we agreed that I would have the sole responsibility of providing for the house. Her parents would buy a three piece suite and we would ask for their help towards the purchase of a washing machine, a refrigerator and a vacuum cleaner, as and when these became necessary. Forty years ago these appliances were considered to be luxury items, so I think this was a reasonable compromise.

In the meantime, Mary's mother continued to stock her daughter's 'bottom drawer' which she started when Mary was only five years old. When we got engaged the 'drawer' was already well stocked but by the time we got married it was more like a well-endowed wardrobe. With the benefit of hindsight I am glad that the generosity of Mary's mother and my own paternal instincts for nest-building were both allowed to express themselves.

During the summer months prior to our marriage Mary's father invited me to join the family for their annual holiday in Cornwall. I was a bit apprehensive because he and I were to share a bedroom. In the event Mr. Lynes treated me as an equal. He was a natural patrician and totally without guile or self-importance. We found that we were both deeply interested in discussing the radical and harsh teaching that was sweeping across the Atlantic from the Brethren hierarchy in the United States. I now realise that we were witnessing the beginning of the change from a benign to a despotic form of leadership amongst the Exclusive Brethren. I will give details of some of the issues and the harsh way non-conformers were dealt with in a later chapter.

Mary's father was a gracious man and he dreaded the prospect of having to sever links with some of his closest friends and relatives who risked excommunication for refusing to comply with some of the more extreme directives of the undisputed leader of the EB's - Mr. Jim Taylor Junior of New York. In the early days of his regime, which he inherited from his father, Jim Taylor tolerated those who questioned his edicts. After a while, however, his closest lieutenants enforced Taylor's teachings, insisting that they were comparable in their authority with those of Scripture itself.

I can only recall two incidents that could have marred those two weeks in Cornwall. Drifting off to sleep on the first night I was dimly aware of a large moth flying around our room. It became, in my dream, a huge seagull and in a state of panic I shook my companion awake, pleading with him to help me evict the invader. We spent at least an hour searching every corner of the room before I was relaxed enough to settle down to sleep. Next morning I apologised for the disturbance but Mary's father just made a joke of the whole thing.

Later on in the morning we made our way to the local Assembly, where it was announced that Mr. Ralph Lynes of Kenilworth would preach their Sunday evening sermon. At his suggestion the elders invited me to preach on the following Sunday.

There are two rules for Brethren preachers - firstly, do not repeat a sermon and secondly, do not use notes. I carefully prepared a new sermon but tucked into my Bible a brief note of the main headings. Mr. Lynes spotted the notes and, at the end of the service, he took me to one side. When I admitted that I had used them he rebuked me in his usual gentle voice, saying that preachers who used notes discouraged the Holy Spirit from speaking through them. It took a few days before our good relationship was restored to its former tranquillity.

# Chapter 19 - The Wedding

The weeks leading up to our wedding were busy ones for both families. The Fear's spent far more money on clothes than they could really afford. I bought my outfit, a double-breasted suit, matching trilby hat and leather gloves from Dunn's, the well-known hatters and gents' outfitters. My younger brother, David, worked for Dunn's when he first left school. On the strength of this, the manager reduced the total bill to £17. Mother made the dresses for Elizabeth and Mary. Both families received a large number of wedding presents. It was long before wedding gift lists became acceptable. These would have seemed presumptuous at the time, so we were still using new pillow cases and towels on our 30th wedding anniversary.

We had originally planned for Mother, James, Mary and I to travel with father in his temperamental twenty-five year old Austin 7 car. However, a group of Brethren in Leicester kindly came to the rescue and accompanied us to the wedding in a hired 40 seater coach. Our formal marriage took place at noon on 28th August 1954 in a civic ceremony at Warwick Registry Office. The legal proceedings were conducted and the marriage certificate signed by a rather tweedy lady Registrar. This was quickly followed by the traditional wedding service at the Kenilworth Meeting Room, where Mary's father was the presiding elder. The pre-arranged ministry was given by the region's top 'ministering brother'. His thirty minute discourse was based on the curious verse in Genesis 29 that says, "When he woke in the morning - it was Leah!". It was as much a mystery to us then, as it is now, how the story of one of the worst instances of trickery in the Old Testament could have any relevance to our marriage!

Following these two ceremonies there was a buffet meal, where a hundred or so relatives and invited guests mingled on the spacious lawn at the front of the house. The wedding guests tucked into the mounds of sandwiches and cakes that had been faithfully piled onto trestle tables by the Kenilworth sisters. It was a rare opportunity to meet new in-laws and renew links with the widespread branches of the Lynes and Line families who had assembled for the occasion from all parts of Britain. Passengers on the top deck of the Midland Red buses that chugged up the hill leading into Kenilworth had a bird's eye view of the proceedings but apart from the photographers there were none of the trimmings associated with non-Brethren weddings. The sisters all wore hats but jewellery and make-up were forbidden. Younger men were distinguished by their Trilby hats and the older men, according to status, by their Homburgs or Bowlers. There was certainly no confetti, music, floral decorations or wine but we thoroughly enjoyed ourselves until the time came for the Bride and Groom to leave for their secret honeymoon destination.

To be honest, our honeymoon was a bit of a disaster! As soon as we arrived in Llandudno it started to rain and at the same time, I discovered that I had left my new leather gloves on the train. Our Bed and Breakfast lodgings were the sort that gave such establishments a bad name. Our third floor room was approached by a narrow, dimly lit staircase. Any movement in the bedroom produced loud creaks. The bed clothes were damp, it was the wrong time of the month and by the second or third day Mary was thoroughly homesick. It was the end of the holiday season so there was very little to do in Llandudno apart from walking in the rain along the pier and promenade, with their shuttered souvenir shops and amusement arcades. Most of the cafes that remained open were of the greasy-spoon variety but as the weather picked up during the second half of the week, so did our spirits. We even laughed at our chapter of accidents and climbed to the top of the Great Orme to enjoy its splendid views of the North Wales coastal resorts.

One of the best things that happened in my life was getting married to Mary. The 19th Century French sculptor, Auguste Rodin, once sent a letter to his wife and it says exactly what I would wish to say to Mary :

*"This letter is just to tell you that my mind is full of gratitude for the greatness of God's gift to me when he put you at my side. Keep this thought of mine in your generous heart".*

# Chapter 20 - Our Family Roots

Perhaps this is as good a place as any to mention the history of our two families. We have gleaned the following from various fragments that have come our way:-

The Fear Family

The earliest member of the family that my sister, Mary, has been able to trace is John Fear, described in the parish register for Knowle, Bristol as a gentleman farmer. He married Alice and they both died in 1546, leaving five children. One of their progeny, also named John, was hung for an unspecified crime in 1607. There are quite a number of other skeletons in the family cupboard!

One ancestor was involved in a bigamous marriage and another married his brother's wife. My own great-grandfather, Daniel Fear, described in the local records as a jeweller, married his first cousin, Eliza Fear. They gave birth to my grandfather, Rufus William, who lived from 1872 to 1947. He was a commercial traveller and his first wife, Annie Jane Haywood, had five children including my father, Paul, who was only six years old when his mother died in 1910.

Grandfather remarried in 1915 and his second wife, Florence Agnes Gooding, bore him three children, Robert Gerald (1916), John Francis (1917-1981) and Florence Elisabeth (1920-1992). We knew them affectionately as Uncle Bob, Uncle Jack and Aunty Betty and we were all delighted to see them, especially as they were much younger than our parents.

Uncle Jack was a firm favourite with us children. We felt we could be ourselves with him, not least because of his boyish sense of humour. We also admired him because of the bravery with which he bore daily insulin injections for the diabetes, which eventually robbed him of his sight.

Aunty Betty, for her part, was always so kind to us and she spent a great deal of her life caring for her elderly parents. Uncle Bob eventually married in 1951 and his wife, Jessie, had a daughter, Margaret, in the following year.

Father's step-brother, our Uncle Bob, was quite a hero to us children. As well as being a schoolmaster he was a gifted preacher and teacher among the Brethren. He also wrote hymns and has kindly given me the following background to the hymn which he wrote whilst serving in the ranks of the Royal Army Medical Corps;

"The poem 'Our God', to which you refer, was written as we set sail from the coast of Britain, in a Landing Ship Tank, at about 7.00 pm on 'D-Day minus 1'. It was Monday June 5th 1944, a glorious summer's evening. What was of immense strength and comfort to me was that I knew the Brethren were gathering in most localities for prayer, though they would be unaware of what was happening. I had a berth below so, when I had watched the coastline recede, I went below. Several were writing letters but I thought that was pretty pointless as prospects of their being delivered were remote - we had only emergency printed Field Letter Cards to use as opportunity arose. I opened my Bible and read Isaiah 40 and that inspired great comfort to my soul. It was then that I wrote my poem;

*He hath fixed the set proportions of the oceans and the land*
*According to the details of His plan;*
*He hath 'measured out the waters in the hollow of His hand'*
*And 'meted out the heavens with His span'.*

*He controls th' unconquered orbit of 'the light that rules the day'*

129

*And guides the myriad worlds that shine at night;*
*And brings forth the host of heaven by their numbers to display*
*The uncontested brilliance of His might!*

*But although His arm is power in the infinite expanse,*
*That same unerring arm is in control*
*To determine and to govern my every circumstance*
*To claim supreme submission in my soul!*

*Yes! And though He counts the nations as 'the dust upon the scale'*
*And soars above their triumphs and alarms,*
*He remembers all about us - that our frame of dust is frail,*
*And holds us in His 'everlasting arms'.*

There were mostly combat units such as commandos on the Landing Ship Tank and we were amongst the medical support. I was one of the two Surgeon's Assistants in a small mobile Field Surgical Unit and our role was to perform surgery on emergency casualties that would never survive sending back along the line. We arrived off the coast of Normandy at first light on D-Day, landed on Sword Beach and, after we had set up, worked solidly on casualties for at least 48 hours (I lost all count of time!) until we were relieved."

A copy of 'Our God' was sent, by somebody, to the Imperial War Museum in London and is now exhibited there in their collection of war poetry.

Uncle Bob also provided me with the following information regarding my father;

"When your father left school, he was apprenticed to a firm of grocers and provision merchants at Redcliff Hill, Bristol. Paul had to be prepared to take on every activity of the trade and it was in the course of delivering goods to a customer by a message-boy's bicycle that he accidentally fell down a flight of stone basement steps. He was in Bristol General Hospital for weeks after that and I remember being very overawed, on visiting him, to see his leg lifted up by traction. They diagnosed a diseased hip bone at that time and it left him lame for the rest of his life."

The Llewellyn Family

My mother's father, Grandfather Llewellyn, was married to Annie Eleanor (nee Coslett) and they had two daughters, Bertha Eleanor and Ruth. They lived in the South Wales mining village of Basaleg. John Llewellyn worked as a Railway Coppersmith. Grandpa Llewellyn must have died at a relatively young age. Annie and Henri Harwood had a son, Vincent, who emigrated with his family to Australia. Granny's second marriage was short lived. She died when she was 77.

The Lynes Family

Mary's father, Ralph Hubert Lynes, married Olive Mary Line in Birmingham in 1933, when they were both aged 24. Their home was in Coventry until it was severely damaged during the 1940 November Blitz on that city. Ralph and Olive subsequently acquired a house on the outskirts of the historic Warwickshire town of Kenilworth. Mary's father managed a chemists shop in Coventry and pursued his profession as an optician.

Ralph Lynes was quite a hard-line member of the Exclusive Brethren and as a leader of the local Assembly in Kenilworth he was frequently invited to minister elsewhere. He was duly accredited for this by the inclusion of his name on what some regarded as the list of Second Division speakers. Although she was always loyal to her husband, Olive, together with her parents and three of Ralph's four siblings, were reluctant adherents of the EB's. One of Ralph's brothers and his two sisters eventually left the movement and were thereafter treated by him as 'outcasts'.

Ralph remarried after the death of Olive in 1980 and he and his second wife, Kathleen, lived happily until Mary's father passed away in 1991.

The Line Family

Mary's grandfather, Walter John (known in the family as 'Jock'), was married to Ethel (nee Owen). They lived in a rambling three storey house in Birmingham and had three children, the eldest of which was Mary's mother, Olive.

Jock, a diploma holding electrical engineer, was a real eccentric with a wide range of interests. He was also possessed with a good humoured cynicism towards the more extreme views of the Brethren. This is illustrated by one of his nieces, Honor Ward. She recalls that, "Uncle Jock was a keen stamp collector and trader. He had the current Stanley Gibbons catalogues on a bookcase beside the fireplace. His son-in-law, Ralph, reproved him, telling him that the books most prominent in the house should be books of James Taylor's teachings (Mr. Taylor being the leader of the Exclusives at that time). Next time Ralph came to call, the catalogues were still there but neatly hidden by a sliding shutter put in by Uncle Jock. This was a joke by Jock who could always see the funny side of Brethrenism."

Mary's grandmother, Ethel, made up for her lack of stature and the loss of one eye (in a railway accident) by her waspishness and lively interest in everything that was going on around her. Jock and Ethel fostered the impression that they had a daggers-drawn relationship but in spite of their occasional spats they were genuinely fond of each other. Both died, virtually penniless, at a grand old age and whilst still in nominal fellowship with the Exclusive Brethren.

The real patriarch and by far the most colourful character of the Line Family was Mary's great-grandfather, Charles A. Line. 'CAL', as he was always known, was the son of the founder of the high class wallpaper and paint manufacturer, John Line and Sons. Expensively produced wallpaper, on which the firm made its name, featured heavily embossed blue and gold paper, in unusually grand designs of urns and curlicues that adorned the walls of many stately homes in Britain. The firm's wallpaper also featured in the Chintz-to-China glossy interior magazines at the beginning of the century.

John Line and Sons, who were later taken over by Sandersons, further enhanced their reputation by pioneering aluminium paints, rather than the more traditional lead based paints. The firm won a contract from the Royal Navy for the sole supply of aluminium paint for camouflaging battle ships during the 1914-18 World War. CAL published pamphlets on lead poisoning which were graphically illustrated with photographs of the crippled hands and diseased jaws of its alleged victims.

Mary remembers visiting her Great Grandfather Line in his Birmingham home which seemed to her to be a splendid Victorian mansion. She particularly remembers that in the entrance hall there was a huge glass case full of stuffed curlews. It was said that one of the long dead birds could be made to move its head by twisting a wire situated underneath the vast showcase.

Charles A. Line was the founder and leader of a splinter group that had broken away from the mainstream of the Exclusive Brethren. His group was known as the Palethorpe Brethren and it had just two Assemblies. One was in Birmingham and the other in Bath. The division occurred over the Eternal Sonship issue, which became a footnote in Brethren history. The controversy was about whether the relationship of Father and Son existed in the Trinity prior to the incarnation of Jesus Christ or only when he entered the human race.

CAL was the author of numerous polemical tracts in which he set out his personal interpretation of Scripture passages which, he claimed, provided evidence of the Eternal Sonship of the Second Person of the Trinity. The magnificently bearded patriarch went to his grave at the honourable age of 93. He was not a man to compromise, so the issue that divided him from most of the Exclusives remained unresolved until the end.

CAL's death left his third wife and three unmarried daughters with the real dilemma of where to hold the funeral service. The service could not be held in the Open Brethren Meeting Room because he himself would have objected most strongly. It could not take place in the Exclusives room for the same reason. Also, if it had been held in the Palethorpe room, the splinter group to which he belonged, all of his male relatives would have boycotted the occasion. In the event, the four ladies made the most sensible compromise. They arranged for the service to take place in their big drawing room which had been cleared so that rows of chairs could be set up for the gathering. The two Exclusive Brethren groups were represented and they were joined by over a hundred relatives and a few friends from the neighbourhood.

Honor, who was also present, wrote that the relatives were all soberly dressed in Brethren style. She added that CAL's widow and three daughters, "sat in the front row in dead black, looking very

Chekhovian. Brethren divisions kept the atmosphere cool. A Palethorpe brother, in his prayer, congratulated the Almighty that, "in the last years of our dear brother's life he was able to gather with that faithful remnant which is meeting in the full light of Scripture" - a phrase very familiar to anyone brought up amongst the Exclusive Brethren".

Honor Ward paid a further visit to her grandfather's house shortly after CAL's death in 1947. Her description of CAL's study is full of interest, "It was the largest and most pleasant room in the house with two or three windows looking out on the laurel bushes and the gravel drive at the front. The room was lined with glass fronted bookshelves and under tables, standing centrally in the room, were orderly piles of books and papers. Among the books we found many different Bible translations and languages for study use, rather than multiple copies of the same printing. CAL was a linguist who read both Hebrew and Greek and this was a scholar's library. On the floor there was a pile of flat cardboard boxes. Each box had a paper label stuck on the exposed end with, in dark blue crayon, writing from his strong angular hand. Several bore the inscription, THE JUDGEMENT OF GOD WILL FALL ON ANY HOUSE HARBOURING THE DOCTRINES TAUGHT IN THESE PAMPHLETS. Grandfather wanted to keep the papers in these boxes as a form of lightning conductor should the Wrath of God strike. They did not contain, as you might expect, any violent attacks on the Christian faith or on morality. Not a bit of it. They contained fairly mild literature from branches of the Exclusive Brethren other than those to which grandfather belonged.

CAL also had in his study a large typewriter, endless stationery and tracts, enormous amounts of filed correspondence from all over the world, numerous rubber stamps and religious stickers. One of the stickers with which he sealed envelopes sent to selected recipients carried the stern warning ABSTAIN FROM ALL APPEARANCE OF EVIL."

Honor adds that in addition to reading books on Christian doctrine and Church history, CAL was an expert on a wide range of social problems and political issues. She notes, for instance, that he was, "very concerned indeed with the fate of the Jews under Hitler, very helpful to Jewish refugees (one of which he employed as a housekeeper) and knowledgeable about the Holy Land, its history, archaeology and present day politics."

Those, then, were the roots and branches of our respective families.

# Chapter 21 - Married Life

Mary and I returned home from our week long honeymoon in Llandudno (North Wales) and it turned out to be something of an anti-climax. My dreams of an idyllic homecoming were less than fully realised.

When I reached for the house keys, Mary's parents burst through the front door to greet us. With the best will in the world they had spent the day cleaning the house and preparing a meal for the four of us. I do not want to sound ungrateful, but I had planned to carry my bride over the threshold before spending a romantic evening alone with her in our first home.

We quickly settled down to a very happy life together. We were pleased with our new house and I embarked on major DIY jobs such as laying a crazy paving patio and path outside the french windows. To do this, we invested in a lorry load of real York paving stone plus a sufficient quantity of aggregate and cement. We also erected wooden fencing to give us some privacy in our small back garden. Mary took responsibility for laying a lawn and planting shrubs around the house. All of these were well established within six months of our taking possession of 'Kenilworth'.

Unfortunately, we made the mistake of buying a Collie sheepdog from a stall in Leicester market. We called him Tigger. It was a stupid choice of breed because, as his name suggests, he had boundless energy and was also rather destructive with our new furniture.

We had the joy of welcoming our first born, Robert John, in October 1955. He was born in a Leicester maternity home. In the 1950's and early 1960's hospitals and nursing homes did not allow fathers to be present at the birth of their offspring. Staff in the maternity wards said that they would be a nuisance, an embarrassment and a hygiene risk. When male obstetricians took charge of difficult births, husbands were kept well away from the delivery room because giving birth was considered to be a secretive and female activity. Even when births took place at home, fathers were merely expected to be on hand to bring kettles of boiling water to the midwife in attendance - this was used for sterilisation purposes. Looking back, I doubt whether I would have been that keen to be present anyway. I am still glad that the miracle of a child's first breath has not been stripped of any of its mystery.

Shortly after Mary brought Robert home we were saddled with a short term resident mother's help. I cannot remember how the system worked but this was something of a Brethren convention and in our early married life we conformed to most of the movement's traditions. She was a grumpy, auburn haired spinster of indeterminable age. She wore button boots, did her hair up in a bun, peered at us through thick rimless spectacles and smelled faintly of lily of the valley perfume. She was an excellent cook and we especially enjoyed her cakes.

Robert was duly baptised, when he was twelve weeks old, 'by immersion' in our bathroom by a saintly old Brother. Mary's diary entry for the day noted the following, "A very good Meeting followed the baptism of Robert John. He behaved very well and was not upset by it. Robert was given a soft blue dog and a pair of rompers."

The arrival of Robert presented us with an unexpected problem. Our Collie dog, Tigger, was probably jealous because when any of us left the room, he jumped on top of our baby son. Obviously we could not let this danger continue so we set out to find a new home for the Collie.

Tigger was an attractive and intelligent dog so we were soon able to find a place for him. His new owner collected him by car and took him five miles to his farm on the opposite side of Leicester. However, Tigger turned out to be an extremely resourceful dog. He must have possessed the instinct of a homing pigeon because a week after he left us he was back on our doorstep, barking with delight and wagging his tail. As you can imagine we could not take the risk of him harming Robert, so with the greatest possible regret we took him to the local vet. This parting was quite a painful episode for us.

Around this time and for some inexplicable reason my abnormal thyroid gland flared into hyperactivity once again. Its stability had been maintained for several years by a carefully controlled regime of drugs and blood tests. The symptoms reached a crisis point when my weight suddenly plummeted. My hands shook so violently that I had to lift a cup of tea or a spoonful of sugar with both hands so as not to spill its contents. The Brethren expressed their concern for my health when they noticed the increasing tremor in my hands and voice when I read out the Scripture passage at the beginning of our Sunday afternoon Bible Reading services.

I was referred back, by my doctor, to the consultant at the Leicester General Hospital who had seen me before at his outpatient clinic. He confirmed that my thyroid gland was malfunctioning. Because of my age (26) he decided against the therapy that involved injections of radioactive iodine. He opted for the less radical surgical procedure that would remove a major part of the diseased thyroid gland in my neck.

A bed on the surgical ward became available within a couple of weeks of that consultation. On the day of admission I went through the usual round of tests. I was blood tested, x-rayed and electrocardiographed. Then my pulse and blood pressure were taken. As soon as I returned to the ward I was examined by a succession of junior doctors who asked me roughly the same biographical questions.

When the consultant turned up for his ward round, he was accompanied by a surgeon and an assorted troupe of junior doctors and medical students. After a cursory examination he called on one of his junior doctors to summarise my clinical history and current symptoms. He ticked off his junior doctor for her failure to identify the tell-tale ridges on my finger nails and seemed totally indifferent to the young lady's obvious embarrassment.

The surgeon returned later in the day and after a careful examination he drew a few lines around the front of my neck in readiness for the next day's operation. The doctor explained that he expected to remove about three-quarters of the thyroid and warned that because it was such a delicate procedure it could involve some risk to my voice box. The anaesthetist also visited me and listened to my heart and lungs through the stethoscope.

After reading my notes and looking at my chest x-ray he explained his role in the operation. The anaesthetist then produced a Consent Form for the administration of the anaesthetic. This included the name, address and phone number of my next of kin. He left with a cheery, "See you in the morning!".

Just before the evening meal Sister came over and said, "Make the most of the meal; it will be the last food you'll eat before the operation and you won't feel like eating anything for several days afterwards".

Before lights-out a male nurse turned up with the necessary items for shaving off all my body hair. He used a cut throat razor and a well lathered brush. Although curtains enclosed my bed, all the patients around me knew exactly, from personal experience, what was going on. When the nurse left, they jokingly pulled my leg and the shared experience seemed to draw me, for the first time, into the typical camaraderie of a men's surgical ward.

When the nurse came round with her drugs trolley she gave me a sleeping tablet and a glass of water. She warned me not to drink anything after midnight. It had been quite a day!

I was woken next morning by the incredible commotion of washing up basins and loud voices. It was still dark outside but the ward was ablaze with lights. I was required to have a bath and told to spit out all the water used to clean my teeth. When I returned there was a prominent notice above my bed that read, "Nil by Mouth".

While the other patients were eating their breakfasts I was issued with a back to front night-gown, a pair of flimsy cotton shorts and a pair of long woollen socks. I was due to go down to the theatre at 10 o'clock so I was sedated with a pre-med injection an hour beforehand. I tried in vain to concentrate on reading the Bible but got into bed when I started to feel woozy.

The next thing I knew was that I was being lifted onto a trolley and then swishing down a corridor beneath a succession of overhead lights. After going up in a lift, I was wheeled into a room where a number of masked figures were milling around in green overalls, trousers and rubber boots. Amid the clatter of steel dishes and instruments the kindly voice of the anaesthetist whispered, "I'm just going to put a mask over your face and by the time we count to twenty you'll be fast asleep".

By the time I got to ten all the lights suddenly went out and when I woke up I was back in the ward with a nurse holding a dish to my parched lips. I later learned that the surgeon had removed over three-quarters of my thyroid gland.

I made a painful but satisfactory recovery from the operation.

# Chapter 22 - Our Children

When Robert was only 15 months old he gave us quite a scare. The youngster must have thought that Mary's iron tablets were Smarties. By the time we realised what had happened he was drifting into a coma, still clutching the empty bottle. We rushed him to hospital just in time for the medical staff to pump out the life threatening substances from his small stomach.

In the autumn of 1956 we were delighted to discover that Mary was expecting our second child. Quite late in her pregnancy Mary had a routine antenatal examination and a blood test taken at the time revealed a potentially serious abnormality. Our doctor explained that the test indicated the presence of what he called 'Rhesus antibodies' in her blood. This was caused by the incompatibility of a little understood factor in our respective blood groups.

The Rhesus (or RH factor), named after the monkey of that name, is present in the main blood groups of 84 per cent of the population and are known by the profession as RH positive. The remaining 16 per cent who do not possess the factor are identified as RH negative. The practical significance of the RH factor arises when an RH negative mother is made pregnant by an RH positive partner. The foetus of such a union is always RH positive. The couple's first baby is usually born without any blood complications but the foetus can pass RH antibodies, through its placenta, into the mother's blood circulation. The circulation could be so affected by the antibodies that the next baby may be stillborn or become jaundiced shortly before birth.

Eventually Alastair went to full term but he was so severely jaundiced at birth that he only survived after he had been transfused with a complete exchange of blood in the maternity department of Leicester Royal Infirmary. Alastair developed asthma attacks when he was about ten months old but apart from those he was a healthy, chubby baby.

For several months before the birth of our third child, Mary's blood was regularly monitored by the antenatal clinic and these tests showed that the number of antibodies had increased. Rather than risk the life of the baby her birth was induced ten days before full term. As a result of this precaution Christine was safely delivered in July 1960 and did not need a postnatal blood transfusion.

Sadly, we were not so fortunate with the birth of our fourth child. This was probably because we had wrongly estimated the actual date of conception. Or was it a hospital blunder? Whatever the cause, when Ruth was born naturally at full term in June 1962, she became so badly jaundiced shortly after delivery that she only lived for a couple of hours. This was a great sorrow for both of us.

Mary was quite understandably grief stricken after the bonding experience of pregnancy and childbirth. After returning from hospital she stayed in bed at home for a few days. During this time Robert, Alastair and Christine stayed with my parents.

Meanwhile I set about arranging for the burial of Ruth's little body. The firm of undertakers, who usually undertook funerals for the Exclusive Brethren in Leicester, was most helpful in obtaining the statutory birth and death certificates. The cause of death entered on the latter was 'Haemolytic disease of the new-born'.

Ruth lay on our sofa and I remember sitting with her for hours during the two days and nights before her burial. We had a night light for company. Ruth had a captivating face and I vividly recall the fragrance of her fair hair and the silky tenderness of her skin. It never occurred to me to photograph our little daughter. She was too sacred for that and I do not think it could have captured the way she looked anyway.

The hospital authorities had asked our permission to carry out a post mortem examination but, as the EB's required the coffin to remain open until the last possible moment, this was not possible.

Early on the day of Ruth's burial the undertaker arrived with a suitably sized coffin. Ruth was laid in it, in a white satin gown, and we drove from the Meeting Room in convoy to the Welford Road cemetery. Even in midsummer it seemed to be a dreary place. It covered a vast area with literally thousands of graves.

A group of us walked from our cars to the freshly dug grave. I was emotionally distraught as I bent down to commit the tiny coffin and its precious contents to the earth and more importantly to the merciful care of our Heavenly Father. There is a particular kind of grief at such a moment and I hurried away so that nobody could see me brushing aside the unbidden tears of self-pity.

The Brethren have a way of trying to reassure those who are passing through difficult circumstances. They say, in a sort of code language, "Look up, it's one of the All Things", which refers to the Biblical promise that, "All Things work together for good to those who love God". However, when a friend kindly squeezed my hand and whispered those words I left the graveside unconsoled.

Later on Mary and I were able to talk about our shared loss and we were really much more consoled by the conviction that a member of our own family had gone to Heaven, before the rest of us. Another Brethren friend assured us that Ruth was better off having been, "released from this present veil of tears". Mary and I both look forward to a reunion with Ruth one day. I cannot remember receiving a bill from the undertakers for the services or the cost of the grave so I can only assume that the Brethren thoughtfully paid for these.

About two years after Ruth's untimely death, Mary was expecting another child. We had been quite encouraged by the news that some hospitals were experimenting with the transfusion of blood while the baby was still in the mother's womb. However, after six months Mary sensed that something had gone wrong. A hospital test confirmed that the foetus was already dead and after an obstetrician had carried out an induction the baby was stillborn. The maternity ward sister told Mary that her premature baby was a perfectly developed little boy. Mary called him John.

I had little realised, at the time, that having a stillborn child is such an appalling bereavement for the baby's mother. Years later Mary was able to talk about the whole range of painful emotions she felt at the time, a mixture of anger, grief and guilt. This was partly because none of her motherly instincts were satisfied by the normal grieving process. It is one of the hidden areas of grief which fathers and others are unable to share. The relationship of a mother with her unborn child is obviously very intimate and exclusive to her.

Perhaps it was too late but, after witnessing the anguish through which Mary had just passed, I resolved she would never face that trauma again.

# PART 5 - A TIME OF CHANGE

Robert, Christine and Alastair

# Chapter 23 - Work and Home

Towards the end of the 1950's a number of major changes took place in our lives. The restlessness that I was feeling about the lack of job satisfaction in my work with the Inland Revenue was intensified when I began to take an interest in international affairs. It was a significant period in contemporary history and yet it was passing me by.

The 1950's began with the Suez Crisis and ended with the birth of Rock 'n Roll in the second half of the decade. Indira Gandhi became India's leader and Fidel Castro swept to power in Cuba. A couple of monkeys became the first primates in space and computers were beginning to play an important role in industrial and medical research. The decade also saw the launch of travel by jet planes and hovercraft along with the sale in shops of colour television sets and pocket calculators.

For some time I had been studying the Jobs Vacant columns in the Leicester Mercury and one job that particularly interested me offered training as a sales representative at one of Britain's leading office equipment manufacturers - Roneo Limited. The successful applicant would be paid a basic salary and given the use of a company car. The advertisement promised that hard work and personal incentive would be rewarded with attractive rates of commission.

I applied for the job and was interviewed by the Sales Manager of Roneo's Leicester branch. He explained that after a probationary period of six months training I would, if successful, be given responsibility for servicing the firm's Accounts in Northamptonshire, the southern half of Leicestershire and Rutland (as it was then) along with the Warwickshire towns of Nuneaton and Rugby. To illustrate this point he ticked off, on his hands, about a dozen of Britain's industrial giants. The projected sales from these Accounts, together with the average quota of new customers, would provide a total income that was 50% better than my present Civil Service salary. He concluded by saying that I could have the job if I accepted in writing within 7 days.

It was not an easy choice. I had to choose between staying in a secure job (that had become a dreary grind of processing tax returns) or embarking on a career that provided much more challenging and rewarding prospects but offered little security for the future. As if to stress the irrevocable nature of the choice the minority who leave government service are required to sign two forms. The first forfeits any entitlement to future employment in the Civil Service and the second requires an undertaking not to breach, at any time in the future, the Official Secrets Acts.

I remember creeping into Robert's bedroom in the middle of the night and asking the sleeping two year old what choice I should make. He seemed such a vulnerable little fellow and I was conscious that his future was as much at risk as mine. Mary had known for some time that I was unsettled and was quite happy about the suggested move. In the event I gave the required month's notice of my intention to resign from the Civil Service.

Within a few weeks of joining the staff of Roneo Limited I felt thoroughly at home and was really enjoying my job. I was trained by a veteran sales representative who had worked for ten years on the territory he would be handing over to me at the end of my probationary period. He not only showed me the product range I would be selling but also introduced me to the buyers and other key personnel who were responsible for purchasing on their company's behalf.

The well-known range of Roneo duplicators were sold by a separate division of the company but I had the job of selling Roneo's wide range of steel office equipment and furniture. Towards the end of my first six month's service I spent a week at the company's London Head Office to learn their procedures for quotations and contracts. At the same time I was being trained to drive a company car and passed the test at my first attempt.

At the end of six months I was happy to sign an employment contract, take delivery of a new Ford Popular car and accept my predecessor's files, as well as taking over his leads for potential new customers. Careful forward planning was essential because buyers of the larger Accounts expected a weekly visit, whereas others required less frequent attention. A good deal of time and effort was needed to develop new Accounts. The value of this new business was one of the ways Roneo's sale management measured the relative performances of its representatives. There was also a financial incentive as new business entitled the representative to a higher initial rate of commission.

I soon realised, after a few weeks on the road, that two types of office equipment manufacturers were in keen competition with each other. The first paid high rates of commission to its representatives but in return expected them to use high pressure techniques to secure as many sales as possible for the firm's products. The after sales service provided by these companies was virtually non-existent. Fortunately Roneo were in the second category. They trained their representatives to build good long term relationships with their customers. The moderate increase in the annual sales targets, set for Roneo representatives, reflected the firm's concern for integrity in the way we conducted business on the company's behalf. Even though these ethical considerations produced lower sales figures in the short term, Roneo's customers remained loyal even when the prevailing economic climate became less favourable.

The conflict between serving the best interests of the customer and obtaining a sale arose because of the wide variety of office equipment available on the market. This applied especially to control systems, that were used for various stock, manufacturing and accountancy procedures. It was our job to help customers through the maze of competing portable ledgers, card filing systems, wall charts and primitive computers.

Shortly after I got the car, I remember one 'never to be forgotten' Tuesday afternoon. After keeping appointments with the two firms in my diary I stopped in the middle of Coalville for a cup of tea. The transport cafe boasted an ancient black and white television set. It consisted of a rather grand wooden cabinet into which was fitted a postcard sized screen. The picture tended to flicker and revolve but it did not matter because, as word spread, the people of Coalville came to the cafe and watched cricket history being made.

It was a ball by ball broadcast of the England v Australia test match in which England's spin bowler, Jim Laker, took all ten Australian wickets. I arrived in the cafe as Australia were resuming their innings after an interruption for rain. They had already scored 112 runs for 2 wickets (both victims of Laker's guile). The sun came out and caused the ball to spin spitefully. Laker took everyone's breath away as he mopped up the remaining eight wickets and England won the Manchester test by an innings and 170 runs. In addition to taking ten second innings wickets, Jim Laker was adding to the nine wickets he had taken in the first innings. With that performance, Laker established his place as the greatest ever off-spin bowler - a record that is unlikely ever to be challenged.

As our family grew and our income increased, we felt able to take out a larger mortgage. In September 1959 we moved into a new detached house that was built to our specification. The house was one of a small crescent of architect designed buildings that backed onto an area of convent owned woodland. Our new house, which cost £3,500, was one of four basic designs offered by a firm of well-respected local developers. The residents in our crescent were middle class and ambitious. They had nicely fitted kitchens and bathrooms, made to measure carpets, central heating and curtains that colour-matched the latest trends of their upholstered furniture.

Nine months after moving into our new home, Christine joined the family and now we were five! It was a welcome change to have a daughter after two sons. This showed when we weighed her down with the names she would have been given had she been first, second or third - Christine Elizabeth and Mary.

# Chapter 24 - Long, Dark Tunnel

In the last few chapters I have tried to remember the sequence in which major changes took place in our lives during the second half of the 1950's. In the midst of these changes we were happy to take refuge in the protective environment provided by the Exclusive Brethren. I was susceptible to flattery and my commitment to the cult grew in direct proportion to the degree of confidence the elders showed in me. On most Sunday evenings I was preaching at small assemblies in half a dozen Leicestershire towns. After a time I graduated to the stage where I was invited to preach at three consecutive Gospel services in our home Assembly in Leicester. The concept of preaching on three consecutive Sundays was based on a precedent said to have been established in the early Church.

It was around this time that a colleague at work gave me an old book of sermons by the 19th Century Baptist minister, Charles Haddon Spurgeon. The reading of books such as this was, of course, forbidden by the Brethren but I devoured every word of it with the intensity of a starving man. Spurgeon brought a blast of invigorating fresh air into my jilted spiritual life. His sermons demonstrated, in the liveliest possible way, that the Gospel related to every aspect of human life. Mr. Spurgeon not only founded an orphanage but he established a theological college for soul-winning students who could not afford the usual fees. One particular sermon in the book introduced me to the world of mass evangelism. It had the strange title, *Moody and Sankey Vindicated*. In it the well-respected Baptist pastor set out to commend the British campaigns of the controversial American evangelist and his song leader at a time when most of his ministerial colleagues were vilifying Dwight L. Moody and Ira D. Sankey.

Most of Spurgeon's sermons were arranged under three alliterative headings. Each sermon was a gold mine that provided me with sufficient material on which to base three 40 minute sermons. I remember one from which I had drawn several generous helpings. The sermon was based on the Genesis account of the creation and the subject so took hold of the congregation that I could see a lively response in their eyes and hear it again at the Prayer Meeting on the following evening.

The impression that I had a toe on the Brethren leadership ladder was confirmed when I received the ultimate accolade of receiving an invitation to a three-day meeting. These occasional gatherings of local Assembly leaders were convened to give a speaking platform to the reigning leader of the Exclusive Brethren. A New York businessman, Mr. Jim Taylor Junior, had inherited the position from his father who had led the EB's for forty years.

This particular three-day meeting was being held in St. Etienne in the south of France. I was deputised to represent our Leicester Assembly, together with the elderly brother (Mr. Burke) who had conducted Robert and Alastair's baptisms. In exchange for the privilege of attending the gathering we were expected to report back any new Assembly Truths propagated by Jim Taylor. In addition to giving two or three major addresses, Mr. Taylor shared his platform with a couple of acolytes. They collectively fielded carefully managed question and answer sessions (Bible Readings). Within a few weeks an edited transcript of these meetings would be published in a book that would be required reading for every family in fellowship with the network of EB assemblies around the world.

The three of us who set off for St. Etienne included Mr. Burke and Mary's father, who represented the Assembly in Kenilworth. We travelled in Mr. Lynes' new car, a French Panhard. About sixty miles south of the Channel port of Dieppe we stopped at a Michelin listed restaurant for lunch. It had been arranged that I would share the driving with my father-in-law. I took over the driving after we had filled up at a petrol station on the main road to the south of France. I will never forget the drama that was soon to engulf us.

The door of the Panhard, which opened from the central pillar of the car, began to rattle as we reached a speed of about sixty miles an hour. It is possible that I attempted to open the door with a view to slamming it shut. In any event the door flew open and, acting like a sail in the wind, caused our car to somersault out of control all over the road. The shock and trauma of being involved in a spectacular traffic accident is clearly etched on my mind. This was before seatbelts were in common use so I was flung violently out of the car.

My first response was one of surprise that I had survived such a horrific crash. Momentarily, as we came to a halt, my life seemed to be hanging by a slender thread as the car threatened to crush the life out of me. During those timeless moments I cried out to God, begging Him to save me and promising that if He would, I would obey the constant pounding to my conscience that had bothered me for the past year. Eventually the battered car rocked back on to its roof only inches away from my helpless body.

As I drifted in and out of consciousness I watched as my two travelling companions scrambled out of the upturned car. Mary's father, who had meticulously planned our journey, instinctively restored calm out of chaos by collecting the regional maps and other papers that had been scattered around the site of the accident. Shortly afterwards I was vaguely aware of the arrival of a siren sounding mini-ambulance and of the excited crowd who helped the driver lift me on to a stretcher.

I next saw Mr. Lynes and Mr. Burke when they visited me in the small rural hospital to which I had been taken after the accident. They were obviously still in a state of shock. I was tearful and full of remorse but they were behaving like a couple of frisky schoolboys. They were sharing a room in a nearby farmhouse. I had received multiple injuries and the extensive areas that had been grazed by its contact with the road had been liberally painted with gentian yellow and my two visitors even seemed to find that rather amusing.

Internal injuries that had not been diagnosed gave me wave upon wave of excruciating pain. Mr. Lynes asked the ward sister whether I could be given a pain killing drug for my upper chest and shoulder injuries. Within minutes of the first injection of a morphine based drug I gratefully succumbed to the euphoria it induced. Little did I know, at this early stage, that as further injections were given on request, I would soon become innocently addicted to these powerful narcotic drugs.

In the meantime news of our plight had reached home and the Brethren at their three-day meeting at St. Etienne. The latter interpreted the accident as an 'attack of Satan' and they assured us of their, 'intercession before the Throne of Grace'. I saw the causes in rather different terms. It seemed to me that my life paralleled the rebellion of Jonah who, because of his failure to obey the word of God, also placed the lives of his companions in peril.

Despite my inconsolable gloom my two visitors always seemed to be in high spirits. They were thoroughly enjoying each other's company and took every opportunity to explore the towns and villages in the region of the hospital.

I could not speak too highly of the kindness of the doctors and nurses. Beds of the dozen patients in my ward always seemed to be surrounded by numerous members of their extended families. I was an object of their curiosity, especially to the children who showered me with fruit.

Life in the rural hospital was enlivened by such treats as a carafe of local wine with every meal. For breakfast and between the main meals we were served with bowls of strong, black coffee that had been generously laced with Cognac. The ward lady, who served this heady brew, came to discover one day that I was British and promised to bring me something special. She subsequently produced a cup of warm water. A small cotton tea bag that was tethered with string floated buoyantly on the surface. Very soon a sort of brown stain seeped from the little bag and weakly coloured the warm water. The lady assumed, apparently, that all Britons pined for a nice cup of tea. I did not have the heart to tell her that I much preferred the strong coffee. From then on I always got the tea.

During these days and long nights in hospital I realised in a fresh way that although I had some strengths I also had plenty of frailties. I was constantly under the lash of a hyperactive conscience and on a roller-coaster of mood swings. I alternated between the confused depression of Job, the penitence of Jonah and the highs induced by the regular morphine injections.

It soon became apparent to my father-in-law that both my physical and mental states were deteriorating. In consultation with the Brethren leaders in London, fresh home from their meetings in

St. Etienne, I was flown to Heathrow Airport, en route for home. It must have been quite an expensive means of transit because the stretcher occupied the space of four passenger seats. It was a painful journey, not least because after several days of narcotic injections I was desperate for another fix. On arrival at Heathrow's medical centre the doctor in charge mercifully gave me an injection to keep me relatively comfortable during the road journey to Leicester.

Within hours of arriving home from France our doctor arranged for my admission to the Leicester Royal Infirmary. It took a simple chest x-ray to show that both of my collar bones (clavicles) had been fractured in the car crash. The broken clavicles were tightly strapped up in a figure of eight configuration. These fractures had been the source of most of the pain. The treatment lessened this so that I was soon weaned off most of the pain killing drugs. A further more sophisticated x-ray revealed that a pulmonary embolism had passed through my lung and heart and had become lodged in an area perilously close to my lungs. Had the embolism not been dissolved, in response to a therapy of anti-clogging drugs, it could have caused a heart attack or a stroke. One doctor said that a heart valve may also have been damaged in the crash, adding that this could be investigated at a later date.

After a period in the LRI I had sufficiently recovered to return home. After all the trauma of the past few weeks it was sheer bliss to sleep once again between the white sheets of my own bed. It was also wonderful to be reunited with Mary and the children in a more normal family environment.

There were, of course, major issues still to be resolved and I will deal with these in the following pages.

# Chapter 25 - Facing a Crisis of Conscience

As I needed a period of convalescence, before resuming my work at Roneo, this gave me plenty of time to reflect on the significance of the unexpected mishap in France. I came to the inescapable conclusion that the car accident was the latest in a series of apparent tragedies which had begun with the loss of our two babies.

We had been brought up to believe that our Heavenly Father lovingly intervened to correct the behaviour of his wayward children. Firmly believing this gave us an explanation for what had been happening. I also believed that I had been granted an opportunity to honour the panicky pledge made during the moments when I faced imminent death in France. Our father frequently exhorted his children to, "Keep short accounts with God". As I confessed to God that these accounts had got into serious arrears, I asked for His forgiveness as I surrendered my life to Him. Although enjoying a sense of God's peace I also knew that, if the slate was to be completely cleaned, I needed to make amends for my past life with the Brethren.

The transaction I had made with God, on that French road, was far too serious to renege at this point. For years I had kept hidden things I knew would get me in trouble with the Brethren, if they had come to light. I mentioned earlier about going to the cinema, watching football matches and flirting with non-Brethren girls. You may think these were youthful misdemeanours but they still hung heavily on my conscience. I also recalled the times when I forgot to take money with me for the Sunday morning collection. Rather than passing the basket on I would thrust a clenched fist through the elasticated hole in the top and drop an imaginary coin into the basket. I fervently hoped that no-one else noticed the absence of a clink as the pretend money failed to land.

It was during this time of heart-searching that I came across a verse in the Letter by James that exhorted his readers to, "Confess your sins to one another".

I felt that the elderly brother who had acquitted himself so admirably in France would treat my confessions graciously. However, I also knew that he was too much of a Brethren loyalist to show undue leniency when a tough rebuke was an appropriate response. I was to see him privately one evening and, as you can imagine, I rehearsed what I was going to say with great seriousness. I poured out my guilty past and not once did he express disapproval. He asked if I had confessed these things to God, adding that I needed no other forgiveness than His. After this I was conscious of a break from the past and asked God to protect me from the natural tendency to be deceitful and hypocritical. Before long this resolve faced a time of severe testing.

As my difficulties became known I was soon a target for the ministry of self-appointed comforters who misrepresented God as a harsh, judgmental tyrant who returned the prodigal to a further period of probation in the far country. Their bitter tone shocked me but I had such an overwhelming sense of gratitude for God's mercy that when their unsigned letters began to arrive I felt no inclination towards retaliation or self-justification. The more they told me that I fully deserved God's judgement the more I wanted to become a channel of God's love and peace.

Meanwhile, Mr. Jim Taylor Junior, the New York drapery manufacturer, was consolidating his Exclusive Brethren Empire. He used entrepreneurial principles to build a pyramid structure of leadership. By this method he could exercise his own authority at every level of management. By the late 1950's the Exclusive Brethren had assumed all the characteristics of a cult.

One of the characteristics of a cult is its ability to keep its adherents preoccupied with the activities of the cult and the teachings of its undisputed leader. The Exclusives qualified on both counts. The feeling of security that comes from belonging to a group of like-minded individuals is a common feature in a Christian cult. C.S. Lewis wrote perceptively on this subject in his *Screwtape Letters* (published by Geoffrey Bles, 1947), ".... All extremes, except extreme devotion to the Enemy (God), are to be encouraged. Any small coterie, bound together by some interest, which other men dislike or ignore, tends to develop inside itself a hothouse of mutual admiration. We want the Church to be small, not only that fewer men may know the Enemy but also that those who do may acquire the defensive self-righteousness of a secret society or a clique. The Church herself is, of course, heavily defended and we have never yet quite succeeded in giving her all the characteristics of a faction; but subordinate factions within her have often produced admirable results from the parties of Paul and of Apollos at Corinth down to the High and Low parties in the Church of England.....".

The place where we met for worship was called The Meeting Room and it was identified outside by a board which read, "God's Word will be preached, DV, every Lord's Day at 6.30 pm. All are welcome". Inside the Meeting Room the atmosphere was austere, with coconut matting on the floor, chairs arranged in square rows and heated in winter by a coke stove.

For most of my first eighteen years I visited our local Brethren Meeting Room at least six days a week. This explains why it has etched such indelible impressions on my memory. There are a couple of things that identify Brethren Meeting Rooms. Three or four small frosted windows are built high up in the walls, reinforcing the impression that these are the premises of a secret society. Two or three small iron plaques state that the buildings are 'Brethren Meeting Rooms for Religious Worship' and they give the telephone numbers of Assembly Elders.

No one who has had an Exclusive upbringing will forget the interior arrangements of the Meeting Room. Ours in Leicester was fairly typical. A heavy half-glazed door led to a small coconut-matted reception area. This area was enclosed by heavy, plum coloured velour curtains which ran from floor to ceiling. In this entrance area worshippers are welcomed with a whispered greeting by a leading brother. Another elderly brother has the job of scrutinising the Letter of Commendation which is required by members visiting from other assemblies. If this failed to satisfy his scrutiny the visitor was invited to join others who were asked to sit behind The Board. The Board instructed visitors not to participate in the Lord's Supper in any way. This was to preserve the exclusive nature of participation, at the Lord's Table, for members in approved fellowship.

Once inside the heavy velour curtains, which excluded all outside traffic noises, the whole atmosphere was one of hushed solemnity. I was not the only one who felt that the inner sanctity of the Meeting Room reflected, for the first few minutes, the spiritual mood that the worshipper brought to it. The Morning Meeting began when the presiding Elder rose to read from the approved Letters of Commendation. We sat in square rows and everybody's attention was focused on the centrally placed linen-covered table on which was laid a cottage loaf of white bread, a silver cup and a small napkin-covered wicker basket.

The ordinance itself, usually called the Breaking of Bread, is marked by the utmost simplicity - the loaf is broken into quarters and then passed from one person to the next, each breaking and eating a fragment from the loaf. A communal cup of red wine is shared by all the worshippers. In theory there was no prescribed sequence to the hymns, prayers and scripture readings but they were all part of the liturgy that had evolved amongst the EB's over the years. Any brother could participate by announcing a hymn or lead in a thanksgiving prayer, but if it strayed from the established liturgical pattern the offending brother was 'corrected' at the end of the meeting by one of the elders.

The offering or collection was given as honoured a place as the bread and wine. It was taken up, without comment, in a covered wicker basket. As a small child I assumed that the money collected was to pay for the bread and the wine. I later learnt that the money would pay for the rent and heating, but was also used to make gifts for travelling brothers who were seen to have a special ministry of disseminating the Brethren leadership's teachings.

Money was also used to subsidise the purchase of monthly ministry books for those that could not afford the full price charged by the Brethren Bible and Tract Depot. After the service the proceeds were counted and entered into a ledger. The notes and guinea coins were then wrapped in a tea towel and banked on the Monday morning. Lesser coins were locked up in the wine cupboard. The Breaking of Bread service concluded with worshipful prayers and hymns from the 19th Century book, *Hymns and*

*Spiritual Songs for the Little Flock.* These were sung at funereal pace and without musical accompaniment.

At the end of the hour long Morning Meeting teenagers scurried around, rearranging the chairs from four square blocks to three or four large circles. A small wooden table, with a glass of water, replaced the larger table on which we had celebrated the Lord's Supper. After this we went home for our Lord's Day lunch. It was there that Brethren exercised the gift of hospitality by seeking out those who would otherwise be eating alone.

We then returned for the hour and a half long Bible Readings which were called Conversational, reflecting the informal atmosphere of these meetings. It would take a more skilful pen than mine to describe them. Compared with the solemnity of the Breaking of Bread, there was almost a party atmosphere in the Bible Readings. Families sat together and although a few leading brothers sat on the front row they were there in quite a subordinate capacity - to keep an eye on things, if you like.

We always started off with a prayer and the reading of a pre-arranged passage of the Bible (taken from the New Version, by the founder of the Brethren, John Nelson Darby). Any brother in fellowship was free to participate. The need for a 'spirit of enquiry' was emphasised so no one could predict the direction the 'enquiry' would take. The least that can be said is that we knew when we had arrived as a good humoured cut and thrust debate was encouraged. If a line of 'enquiry' came into close proximity with any aspect of 'new Assembly truth' we pursued it with ill-concealed enthusiasm. This was the environment where apprentice leaders and the more inhibited young brothers were encouraged to develop their gifts. Of all religious services I have ever attended the Brethren Bible Reading was quite unique!

After the Bible Reading we had time for a cup of tea and the rearrangement of the chairs from broad circles to straight rows. A small wooden pulpit, adorned with a Reading Bible and carafe of water, stood at the front for the use of the preacher. Immediately before the 6.30 p.m. Gospel Service a few of us huddled for a prayer meeting, asking the Lord to bless the strangers who came under the sound of the Gospel message. A few of the younger brothers stood outside offering invitation leaflets to folks who were passing by the Meeting Room.

We expected little and received even less of a response.

# Chapter 26 - Family Holidays

During the children's school years we usually took two weeks holiday away from home. Only the wealthier families could afford to take their holidays overseas and even continental package holidays were regarded as a luxury.

In common with most families we were perfectly content to enjoy a seaside fortnight in one of Britain's many coastal resorts. Like our parents we hired an on-site caravan or a self-catering flat. We took a different place each year and part of the thrill was discovering our holiday home and its surrounding area.

The usual objection to taking self-catering accommodation was that it allowed mother insufficient opportunity to escape from her usual household chores. I am not sure whether we were just following a Brethren custom or if we did it on our own initiative, but we responded to this challenge by drawing up our family job rota. This was mutually agreed during the week before our holiday. We did not consult mother except to ask her to wash and iron our clothes. I took responsibility for shopping and the cooking of our main lunch meal.

With few exceptions we spent the morning on the beach. I left the family mid-morning and we met for lunch at about 1 o'clock. I thoroughly enjoyed my particular job of getting lunch, not least because of the variety of shops that were offering local produce. We did all the washing up and made our beds before setting out for our chosen afternoon trip. We toured around the area visiting places of local interest. On the way back to our digs we patronised a fish and chip shop and stopped off for a picnic before the meal got cold. If we were on a caravan site Robert and I replenished our stocks of water from the camp toilet block. The three children prepared our simple breakfast and loaded up the car with the items we needed for the beach. The sun always seemed to shine all day during our summer holidays with rain only falling at night. Most people of our age say the same!

On some days Robert, Alastair and I left mother and Christine to their own pastimes, collecting shells or drawing birds, whilst we set off on our own adventure. I was probably a poor role model for the boys because I was distinctively drawn to anything that was slightly conspiratorial or in dubious taste. This was certainly true of a hobby that we relentlessly pursued for three or four years.

The interest was sparked when we paid a routine visit to a gents' public toilet on the promenade at the resort where we were staying. This was the town that boasts itself as the Queen of the English Riviera. The toilet was in a disgusting condition lacking even the most basic facilities. There was no attendant to whom we could complain so on the following afternoon we presented ourselves, all fired up, at the local tourist office.

I introduced myself to the harassed looking lady behind the desk as an 'Inspector of Taxes from Leicester'. We soon found ourselves facing an elderly man across the desk. We had composed a speech overnight. It noted that this resort depended on tourism and provided a wide range of hotels, restaurants and coach outings. We had intended a dramatic pause at this point. I was rather flustered and the official was so obviously on the defensive that I just blurted out, "You should be ashamed of yourself because the men's lavatory at the end of the pier just stinks!". He was all I pictured a local official should be, courteous and wing-collared. After asking if we would like a cup of tea and us accepting his surprise invitation, he said that he could not comment because he had never visited the premises, adding that he had very limited funds to improve the facilities. Over tea and biscuits he agreed that an impression such as ours would be unlikely to improve the tourist trade. Our new found friend promised to get a Council official to send him a report on our complaint. As we shook hands he invited the three of us to visit him again before the end of our holiday.

We visited the official again before the end of the week. In the meantime he had carried out some research into the history of what he, somewhat delicately, described as your 'gentlemen's urinal'. He said that the curator of the local museum had revealed that it was a listed building. We later discovered that the museum planned to restore the porcelain fittings, mosaic floors and brass pipework to its former glory. I am not sure where this information came from, but it is gratifying to know that our humble researches had led to more than just the provision of improved facilities for visiting tourists.

# Chapter 27 - Leaving the Exclusive Brethren

This will be the most difficult chapter in the book to write, not least because of the difficulty of explaining how we had become so imprisoned by the EB system. In many ways it was so rational as we had been brought up to be compliant and were willing to be totally subservient.

The church in Britain has had a tradition for independent groups that breakaway and develop independently of the established church. These movements have often been born out of dissent, e.g. the Puritans, Wesley and the Methodists, Charles Spurgeon within the Baptists and Darby leading the Brethren Movement.

A careful review of a number of religious groups and denominations will often confirm the proposition that, "every human institution tends to reproduce its opposite within two or three generations of its beginnings". In any event this theory is well illustrated in the 150 year-old history of the Exclusive Brethren. Everything within the system is committed to the elimination of the clerical system.

By the 1950's sole and absolute authority was invested in an individual who came to be recognised as the Universal Leader of the movement. Acceptance of his apostolic teaching and discipline became a condition of membership within the Exclusive Brethren. He enforced his leadership by appointing a network of loyal apostles to whom he delegated his authority at a regional level. Generally speaking the Exclusives reject the majority of Spirit-endowed gifts such as prophets, pastors and evangelists but recognise, in principle, the gift of 'apostle', which they interpret as ordained solely by God i.e. a theocratic apostleship. An apostle delegated his authority, as St. Paul did, when he appointed someone to oversee a particular region.

The ministry of the Universal Leader spawned a library of books which were regularly distributed by the in-house EB publisher - the Stow Hill Bible and Tract Depot. These books propagated the distinctive and revised interpretation of Scripture by the current leader and were required reading within the households of all members. The body of teaching contained in these books became known as 'new Assembly truth' and dealt with every conceivable aspect of the lives of members. These included relationships, finance, dress, education and employment. Failure to accept and comply with the arbitrary rules, legislated by the leadership, led to the imposition of a range of disciplinary measures, including the ultimate sanction of excommunication.

Earlier I briefly traced the Brethren movement in happier times, before autocratic leadership ruled in the EB's and led to the tragic consequences that inevitably followed. It is now public knowledge that those who dared to dissent against such extremist teachings were summarily excommunicated, even when this resulted in shattered lives, broken families and suicides. In retrospect I am prompted to ask why the authorities, at least in Britain, failed to act with greater vigilance when such basic human rights were so seriously violated. For instance, the courts failed to protect minors when they were forcibly removed from the care and custody of their parents. The Charity Commissioners granted favourable tax concessions on the payment of internal gifts and the rating authorities exempted Brethren from paying rates on their Meeting Rooms, even when these premises ceased to qualify as 'places of public worship'.

At one time the EB's shed about a tenth of its membership over what was referred to as, 'the ministry of the Holy Spirit'. Anyone who failed to acknowledge the distinctive place of the Holy Spirit was held guilty of 'grieving the Holy Spirit'. It occasioned the publication of a new edition of *Hymns for the Little Flock*. The counting of heads was strictly discouraged but it was estimated that the total world-wide membership was in the region of 10,000. There were only negligible additions through conversions, by far the greatest growth came through births.

I now use the word cult rather than sect as a better name for this group, because they exhibit characteristics such as expelling dissident members and assuming that God's blessing is solely reserved for the leaders and adherents of its rules. This is the situation faced by those who are 'put out'. Like other cults they emphasise doctrine that the mainstream Christian denominations regard as central in the creeds of the Church. The Exclusives, however, allowed Biblical authority to be eroded and Jim Taylor Junior's teaching to take precedence over Scripture in basic matters of belief and practice.

At the end of the 1950's Jim Taylor Junior dropped a bombshell in the midst of the EB's that had a devastating effect on the whole cult. It started when he declared, at a three-day meeting, that members would no longer be permitted to eat a meal or have a cup of tea with anyone outside of the fellowship. Taylor argued that this new prohibition would simply strengthen the central tenet of the Brethren teaching, 'Separation from the world'. His scriptural basis for the new ruling was extremely tenuous and to be found in 2 Timothy 2 v.19-21, J.N. Darby (JNB) translation;

*".......The Lord knows those that are his. Let everyone who names the name of the Lord withdraw from iniquity. In a great house there are not only gold and silver vessels but also wooden and earthen, some to honour and some to dishonour. If therefore one shall have purified himself from them, he shall be a vessel to honour, sanctified, serviceable to the Master, prepared for every good work.*
"

Some thought that Taylor was caught unawares by the backlash that this provoked. Those who were aware of the clever way he controlled the movement knew that he was neither unintelligent nor theologically illiterate and had carefully calculated the effect it would have. He contributed to the growing ferment by devoting a book of his ministry to what became known as the 'eating issue'. He made it a test of loyalty to his leadership. I suspect that he and his leadership team had earlier detected a growing dissident element that posed a threat to the Taylor dynasty.

This new teaching failed to harmonise with the spiritual instincts of the people. It created a culture of deceit that began to eat away at the moral fibre of the Brethren. Dissent was suppressed and membership of the Brethren was decimated. In the process the dissident element was purged either by voluntary defection or expulsion. Taylor claimed that the Brethren had been cleansed but he cynically disregarded the immense suffering that followed in the wake of his decrees. Hundreds of people were cast aside by savage acts of excommunication whilst hundreds of homes were divided.

Some of the cases began to appear before the courts whilst others were featured in the press.

Splits and schisms were already endemic but the Exclusive movement had now become more introverted, stressing separation not only from the world but from other Christians. All members are expected to have unwavering allegiance to the cult. Indeed, submission to the leaders involves being a slave to the system and its rulers. The rule is to learn to obey. You have to learn to follow only God and his anointed leaders. This means the voluntary abandonment of individualism and self-interest, so as to freely choose submission to God's chosen leader. Any sign of insubordination is seen as rebellion not only against delegated authority but against God Himself. This system involves the acceptance of admonition and correction, to be determined by local appointed elders.

An average sized assembly was cared for by two elders, one of whom had pastoral/priestly qualities. An elder was usually consulted if someone had absented themselves from meetings. A network of 'heads of households' were called to visit these potential delinquents. The system of discipline used by the Brethren was based on the formula outlined in the New Testament passage from Matthew 18 v 15-17, (JND translation);

*"But if thy brother sin against thee, go, reprove him between thee and him alone. If he hear thee, thou hast gained thy brother. But if he do not hear thee, take with thee one or two besides that every matter may stand upon the word of two witnesses or of three. But if he will not listen to them, tell it to the assembly and if also he will not listen to the assembly, let him be to thee as one of the nations and as a tax-gatherer."*

Those who fail to be broken in total surrender to the authority of the leaders are regarded as showing the hallmarks of the world, i.e. pride, rebellion and the secular trends of an independent and individualistic spirit.

It is an understatement to say that it was difficult to leave the EB's. This is true of all deeply committed religious groups. They keep adherents in constant fear of the outside world and of exposure to the attacks of the Devil. Some relative newcomers are dismissed as spiritual dilettante but more established members face a barrage of threats that may involve legal proceedings over property and job, as employment and mortgage were often provided by Brethren businessmen. Family wrangles can be bitter and leaving involves ostracism.

We little expected that our ultimate deliverance from the EB's would come as the result of a new directive from the New York leadership. Even some of the most ardent of EB loyalists were casualties because of its conflict with evangelism.

Our disenchantment with the Exclusive Brethren was gradual as we detected extreme legal teaching creeping in with a loss of missionary and gospel outreach. The Lord had been convicting me over a period of three or four years, but it was a big step to leave relatives, friends and fellowship, especially as we were told that there was no spiritual life outside the Brethren. We were about to leave those whose insight and concern I highly esteemed, but we were given strength as God chastened us through the deep sorrow of the near fatal car crash and the loss of our baby. God had spoken through these circumstances and I was too frightened not to listen and obey the awesome voice of God to my heart, mind and conscience.

We had hoped that our exit would be a smooth one but in our different ways we were all fraught with emotion. As far as we are able to recall our two youngest, Alastair and Christine, came through the experience virtually unscathed. We had thought, until recently, that Robert had been badly confused by the disturbance through which we all passed. He was by now expected to take quite an active part in Brethren activities, i.e. participating in public prayer and reading of the appropriate scripture passages. He seems to have taken their harsh treatment in good part, although his exclusive grandparents tried to persuade him to remain in the assembly after we left. I heard them once threatening him that he would never see his grandparents again if he left the fellowship with his parents. It was probably Mary who was most deeply affected by the disruption in our family life. She needed tranquillisers for a while to cope with all of this. All five of us escaped to a wooden chalet in a quiet holiday resort in rural mid-Wales.

On our return we had to contend with many visitors, both family and friends, seeking to persuade us to stay within the Exclusives and accept their doctrine. We were kept in a state of spiritual quarantine. 'Under discipline' was the phrase used for someone suspended because of their questioning. Some were winsome voices of our esteemed parents and stalwart friends who urged patience and pleaded with us not to, "kick against the pricks" or, "resist the voice of the Holy Spirit".

Towards the end of this period Mary had a deep spiritual experience causing her to 'fall in love with Jesus' - her words. We also met Christians from a nearby Open Brethren church with whom she eventually broke bread. No longer would the Exclusives wait for us.

The actual meeting in which the judicial process of excommunication reached its climax was the Care Meeting. The evidence of witnesses and the case for the prosecution, however, was given a good airing at the preceding Monday Prayer Meeting and the Wednesday evening Bible Reading. I lacked the courage to attend the crucial Care Meeting in which the final curtain was drawn on our lifelong membership of the EB's. As we did not attend a judgement was arrived at in our absence and we were 'withdrawn from' or excommunicated. A typical verdict was known to include a statement such as, "their action has the smell of sulphur about it", i.e. the smell of Hell.

This was a total break and very traumatic. Many ex-EB's have been known to leave Christianity after such an experience. There was for a long time a cloud of sadness over our lives but there were glimmers of light that beckoned us to stumble on through this long, dark tunnel.

Like all Exclusive Brethren I had become addicted to imbibing the teachings of Brethren leaders. I missed the monthly volume of Jim Taylor Junior's ministry that were churned out by the Stow Hill Bible and Tract Depot. Only later did I realise that these had quite an insidious influence on our lives.

Now, as I travelled the country for my work, I sought out second hand bookshops and became acquainted with the fascinating world of religious books. My original researches were a little frustrating because Spurgeon's sermons from which I had, clandestinely, derived a great deal of spiritual help were in short supply. The renowned Victorian was, however, well read and frequently referred in his sermons to other preachers to whom I eagerly turned. To be honest I was quite undiscriminating and anything that had a spiritual ring to it I bought. It does not seem to have done me a great deal of harm!

It would be difficult to describe the pleasure that I derived from collecting Christian books and the time soon came when I decided to burn my entire Brethren library of several hundred titles. This became for me a sort of sacramental rebirth - a quite significant and radical change in my reading habits.

# PART 6 - BILLY GRAHAM

John Fear - Exclusive Pedigree

# Chapter 28 - Salesman of the Year

Not surprisingly, after all that I had experienced, I was very slow to involve myself in the life of the church outside of the Brethren. I suppose that I had been so thoroughly brainwashed that I genuinely believed that there was no spiritual life in the world apart from the Exclusive Brethren meetings.

After our excommunication from the EB's I was visited on more than one occasion by the elders from a nearby Open Brethren Assembly. They were most gracious and made it clear that if I would like to attend their meetings I would be more than welcome. For a long time I was suspicious of their motives and kept these kind folk at arm's length.

James Taylor had been vitriolic in his condemnation of the Open Brethren because of their alleged compromise with the world and the 'apostate church' at large. I had been taught from my youth that the Open (or Christian) Brethren were, in Mr. Taylor's words, "the dirtiest ditch in Christendom". I passed this comment onto the Brethren representatives who visited me. They just smiled and said they did not mind what I thought of them as long as I knew that my fellowship would be valued if I cared to come to the meetings at any time.

Eventually their kindness won me over and I began to go to the little Brethren Assembly near to our home. The order of service was not as strange as I had thought. They followed a fairly similar pattern of meetings to those I had known in Exclusive days. Nevertheless I lost no opportunity to express my criticism of everything they did, because I probably felt myself to be far superior spiritually. The elders responded by entrusting me with small tasks. One of these was to attend an exploratory meeting in Nottingham to discuss the possibility of holding Billy Graham Television Relays. A team member came to enthuse a group of ministers with the concept of Closed Circuit Television relays from London. This caught my imagination, as it was all so new to me, but the group of 80 ministers were not so excited.

I returned to Leicester and found a suitable place, the Granby Halls, which would seat 7,000 people. I received a quote to book the venue for 10 nights. As it was free for the period in question, I signed the contract and reported to the Billy Graham team member that this had been organised. On reporting back to the elders, I told them that I was absolutely sure that this was of God and it was not a big deal. Very graciously they told me that I had exceeded my authority and that I was on my own. They suggested I should contact other ministers in the city. I got in touch with the assistant minister of Melbourne Hall (a free church) who was almost as horrified as the elders because the church in Leicester was totally fragmented.

At this stage I began to get concerned. We made a list of ministers and other active Christians who were invited to a meeting. They came and listened to my vision and began to catch a glimpse of the opportunities that could arise from such a venture. Nottingham heard about this and said, "Let's make it an East Midlands Crusade". I wrote later about this important time and so include the article below:-

The most unforgettable chapter in my life by John L. Fear

(Republished from The Christian, July 15th 1966)

In the autumn of 1963 I left the fellowship of a Christian community which strongly disapproved of the preaching of Billy Graham, and because of its exclusivist emphasis on 'separation from the world' had virtually no evangelistic outreach and in consequence none were added to the existing membership. This was a big step, as apart from my business colleagues, we had no associations outside of this circle and were ignorant of the doctrinal position of the various churches around us.

It was a wonderful thrill to discover light and life instead of the threatened darkness and deadness. In addition we were given a cordial and sympathetic welcome by Christians we had previously maligned. This more than compensated for being ostracised by our 'exclusive' relatives and friends. In the months that followed I experienced great liberty and joy in preaching and in the other areas of service that opened up. One of the most absorbing interests was in the field of Christian literature. Previously my reading had been restricted to the ministry published by the Stow Hill Bible and Tract Depot. I enthusiastically set about replacing this library with over 1,000 books by C.H.Spurgeon, F.B.Meyer, D.L.Moody, Bishops Ryle, Moule and other like-minded ministers of the Word.

At the beginning of 1965 I felt a great urge to be free of secular employment and money-making so that I could exercise, in His service, the organising gift that the Lord had given me. In the months that followed I feverishly searched around for some avenue of full-time service and replied unsuccessfully to advertisements in the Christian press. One door after another closed until I restfully accepted that the Lord would reveal His perfect will at the right time.

As a result of a car accident in 1962 I was awaiting surgical treatment in a London hospital to correct a heart defect. The cardiac specialist, in the meantime, advised me to lead a leisurely existence, retiring to bed at 8 o'clock each evening.

In June 1965, I clearly discerned the call of God fully to commit myself to the proposed Television Relays of the Billy Graham Greater London Crusade to the East Midlands. When I was invited to serve in the capacity of Secretary of the Executive Committee I hesitated, before accepting, because of my heart condition and business commitments. Briefly on the health aspect, I have experienced almost complete relief from abnormal fatigue during the months of preparation, despite long hours spent in working, travelling and attending meetings. Although I have lost some weight my doctor has expressed surprise at the general improvement in my condition.

I will now attempt to give an account of the truly wonderful way that the Lord has undertaken for me in business. On accepting responsibility for the crusade work I soon realised that at times it would be so demanding as to make it necessary to devote much time to it during normal business hours. As a salesman it is quite easy to take time off without anyone knowing - supervision is minimal and for this reason selling attracts quite a high proportion of work-shy people. However, as a Christian I know that God would not honour deceit and I had the most definite impression, as I prayed over the problem, that if I did God's work that He would do mine. I have since proved in the most unforgettable chapter in my life that He is a far better salesman than I will ever be.

For the past 10 years I have covered the same territory for my present employer. My highest sale figure for any one month had in this period been just over £4,000 - this at a boom time. Business was now rather slack owing to economic uncertainties and all my colleagues were producing poor figures. I had been given a sales target (or quota) of £3,000 per month. In November crusade activities were particularly heavy and I was only able to spend a maximum of three days a week selling. The staggering fact was that orders poured in at an unprecedented rate and the total sales for the month exceeded £7,000!

This not only amazed me but everyone including the Regional Manager, who knew that I was spending a good deal of time on crusade preparation. Orders came in the post unsought and totally unexpected. Some were for complicated office systems that normally would have taken days to negotiate and others from difficult customers who in the past had only ordered after lengthy consideration and some persuasion. In this particular month I quoted for a large contract for a nationalised industry. We had previously been unsuccessful in obtaining a contract in these circumstances (we only quote as a courtesy), because they are always decided on price and we produce equipment at the expensive end of the scale. After one thirty minute interview I was handed the contract and left competitors' representatives hopefully sitting in the reception area.

At the regional sales meeting in January the sales performances for the preceding six months are reviewed. This revealed that my sales figures were 32 per cent above the target set and the other 11 representatives from 2 per cent up to 45 per cent down. The sales manager, who is a rather hard-boiled cynical type of executive, asked me what had happened to my territory. When I said that prayer had brought in the business, he replied, "Well if you can pray it in, there is no need to work". In January and February sales on my territory were £4,700 and £5,200 respectively, and I proved that the more time I spent on crusade business the better the figures were.

At the beginning of March a national sales competition was launched. This meant that more than a hundred salesmen throughout the country would be competing for the first prize of a luxury holiday in Majorca for two, with all expenses paid and a generous spending allowance. In the Midlands we have never done very well in this type of competition - staff in London have great territorial advantages. At best in previous years I have ended up around the middle of the table. This competition was to last twelve weeks and points were awarded for certain items of equipment which were not currently selling well. At no stage in this competition was I placed lower than fourth and, although I am still awaiting announcement of the final result, it seems very probable that I have won first prize.

Typical of what happened throughout the twelve weeks is reflected in the pattern of the last two days. The regional and sales managers were so excited at the prospect of one of their own men winning that they offered to spend the last few days visiting customers on my territory in an attempt to secure more business - at the end of their effort they had not obtained a single point! I spent the penultimate day striving very hard and travelled long distances - no success. On the last day, having learnt the lesson of complete dependence (I felt very rebuked at not having wholly trusted the Lord and attempting in my own strength to assist Him in what he was doing), I spent the day restfully at the office and the orders just flooded in by post and telephone. The office staff were only just able to keep pace with the recording of them. Orders for that one day alone equalled those obtained by over seventy

186

*representatives during the entire twelve weeks. I felt overwhelmed with thankfulness to a loving and faithful God.*

The above was the first time a piece of mine was published in the Christian press and I read it several times with relish. The outcome of the competition was that I had won the Salesman of the Year prize and we thoroughly enjoyed our all-expenses paid holiday in Majorca. During the six nights of the crusade, the aggregate number who attended the television relays at the Granby Halls in Leicester exceeded 35,000. Of these up to 2,000 made a spiritual response i.e. came forward as enquirers for counselling at the evangelist's nightly appeal. I have had the privilege of meeting a number of these who have since gone into full time Christian work or undertaken theological training for the ministry. We met our budget of about £10,000 before the end of the crusade. This came from supporting churches in the mainstream denominations and individual supporters.

The local newspaper sent a photographer on the second night of the relays. He persuaded me to stand in front of the Granby Halls holding a board, with the chalked notice, FULL UP. Incidentally, when I resumed full time work with Roneo, the sales resistance resumed its normal pattern. I had to work just as hard as before to acquire the sales quota that had been established for my territory.

At this point I was faced with a further dilemma. Our Regional Manager invited me to accept promotion to the position of Sales Manager for the East Midlands area. On the same day I received a letter from the EA (Evangelical Alliance) asking if I could meet their General Secretary, with a view to joining their staff at the earliest possible date. During the same week I also heard about the possibility of joining the Billy Graham team on a permanent basis.

# Chapter 29 - CCTV's in 25 Centres

When Billy Graham heard about the procedures we had used in Leicester, for the 1966 CCTV (Closed Circuit Television) relays in the Granby Halls, he suggested that a similar programme could be applied in the 25 cities that had agreed to participate in the relays in 1967, when Billy Graham returned to Earls Court for a nine-day crusade.

Some cities had to be turned down because there was not enough equipment to go round. The Christian newspaper covered the whole story. This is an extract:

*"On January 12th John Fear went to London from Leicester to act as co-ordinator for the relay centres. His business enterprise and clear vision of what had to be accomplished transformed what might have been a nightmare into a working possibility. Crusade Director, Bill Brown, welcomed him with open arms.*

*As he worked his way around the centres in the early days John found many problems unresolved. He told one committee, "Brethren, you ought to be ashamed at the lack of progress you have made. If I were in your shoes I would ask God to forgive me for the state we are in." Within two days the situation was transformed and progress thereafter was remarkable. In detailed bulletins John communicated with the centres each week and even he was surprised at the way in which centres, in general, kept pace with each other. The outline had been given to each, but the nationwide unity of purpose encouraged John to believe that there was more to this than human planning."*

During the mission week there was a control centre at Earls Court with open phone lines to each relay centre. The report goes on...

*"From the first night the message was the highlight of the programme. The preliminaries were professional and trimmed to fit an agreed schedule, and many time proved moving. But the authority and simplicity of the Gospel address night after night always went further and deeper and the response was tremendous.*

*By mid-crusade, centres were sending for more counselling materials and the night by night reports to John Fear, stationed in Earls Court, became more and more enthusiastic. The reception in each centre was superb. Reporters covering the crusade in half a dozen centres all formed the opinion that the crusade was more effective on the screen than in the vast arena of Earls Court. First class camera work and the evident sincerity of all taking part on the platform made up a convincing ninety minutes of evangelism."*

The most enduring pop singer during the second half of the twentieth century was Cliff Richard. During the early days of the Earls Court Crusade in 1966 I was invited, along with representatives from other relay centres, to attend the crusade services and seats were reserved for us on the platform. I was surprised when Billy's song leader (Cliff Barrows) invited me to meet Cliff Richard in order to escort him onto the platform to give his first public testimony. The news of this had obviously leaked out because a fair number of those attending the meeting carried placards with photographs and slogans that were intended for such an occasion. The Press, represented by photographers and reporters, were also there in strength.

Cliff had been converted to Christianity about two years earlier, but his spiritual counsellors had urged him not to make this publicly known until he was more mature in his new found Christian faith. Prior to walking to the platform from a small cubicle where Cliff

Barrows had left him with me, he told me how nervous he was at the prospect of giving his testimony to such a large gathering and how it would be treated by the press representatives who were there. After tuning his guitar, Cliff asked if we could pray together for the Lord's help in the half hour that lay ahead of him.

When Cliff left his home in India, he was seasick for most of the three week voyage from Bombay. His family had a few suitcases and just five pounds between them. For the first months all five of them huddled together in one small room but eventually they saved enough to pay the rent on a small house. Cliff hated England and everything about it. He loathed exams, was miserable when children made fun of his red and swarthy face and he never adjusted to the cold, sugarless milk he was forced to drink at school.

Life, however, took on a new dimension when Cliff saved like mad for an Elvis Presley album. He was fourteen and with the record player turned to full blast he spent hours in front of the mirror, miming to the album and mimicking all of Elvis's distinctive movements. Cliff gave his first pop performance at his local youth club accompanying Elvis numbers with a guitar bought by his father for £2. Quite soon Cliff and his group, The Drifters (later renamed The Shadows), were getting bookings to sing rock and roll music in dance halls and clubs. The breakthrough came when they were spotted by a recording agent at a talent contest.

Cliff took some hard knocks at the beginning but within a year he had signed a professional recording contract and there were concert tours, television, films and what the media called Cliff-mania. The story of how Cliff leapt from teenage obscurity to the popularity that got him voted 'The World's No. 1 Male Singer' is now history but suffice it to say that he has made over a hundred singles, of which twelve were number one hits, and produced a score of albums.

From all this he has earned an estimated fifty million pounds, but Cliff Richard has shared some of his immense wealth with many, around the world, who are suffering hardship and despair. An interesting example of his compassion took place during a visit to Haiti. There he met a poverty stricken mother and her small son. From then until now he has adopted them as his own family. Cliff would insist that he is only human but his concern for others and generosity provide an eloquent witness to God's love in action.

# Chapter 30 - Joining the Billy Graham Team

Towards the end of the 1967 All-Britain Crusade I heard from Cliff Barrows that Billy Graham was wanting to spend a day with me to discuss how I could be involved with his team on a longer term basis.

The initial invitation, extended to me in August 1966, was for the six months needed to assist the team in its preparation for the Earls Court Crusade and extended by CCTV to 25 other cities throughout the UK. I was therefore surprised to hear on the day following the crusade (in July 1967) that Billy Graham had taken a flight home to the United States on the previous evening. This was apparently a policy decision on his part to depart from the city in which he had been leading an evangelistic crusade, so as to discourage the formation of an ongoing church by the new Christians and the rank and file of Billy Graham's crusade supporters.

While we were closing down the crusade headquarters office, which we had established at Piccadilly Circus in London, I was asked to join the British Evangelical Alliance. Their General Secretary explained that my duties would include the formation of local EA regional offices who would co-ordinate the ongoing work of crusade follow up and the work of evangelism in the 25 cities that had participated in the CCTV relay programme.

The Board also invited me to consider taking responsibility for the EA file which had been opened for the management of funds sent by supporters for Third World Relief. Several hundred pounds had been designated for this purpose during the period of the crusade. It seems that these funds were donated quite spontaneously in response to the sense of spiritual expectancy that had been generated through the counsellor training programme and the setting up of hundreds of prayer groups throughout the areas covered by the relays. A member of the Board had already suggested that this fund should be known as The Evangelical Alliance Relief Fund - this was an inspired title for the fund and it is known as TEAR Fund to this day.

I was immensely flattered to be offered this responsible appointment, but I felt uneasy about the move away from direct evangelism that such a radical change would have involved. The Evangelical Alliance was founded in 1846 and exists to be the corporate voice of evangelical Christians in Britain. The Alliance aims to generate understanding and co-operation between Christians of all denominations in a variety of Christian, political and social initiatives. An evangelical is described, in an EA handout, as a person who has, "committed his or her life to Jesus Christ and seeks to live under His Lordship and authority, believing and accepting the Bible for what it says".

At about the same time as I had received this invitation from the EA, a letter from Billy Graham's Administrative Director asked if I would be free to join the team on a permanent basis. He invited me in the same letter to visit the United States for further discussions.

The programme for this visit was planned by Billy Graham's Business Manager. In addition to visiting the headquarter offices of the BGEA (Billy Graham Evangelistic Association) in Minneapolis, I spent some days at the team office in Atlanta, Georgia and a brief period with associate evangelist Leighton Ford (he was married to Billy's sister Jean in Toronto, Canada). He was a greatly gifted evangelistic preacher in his own right and was expected to give leadership to the BGEA when Billy Graham ceased his worldwide ministry. During this visit to the United States I also spent ten days, as Billy's guest, at his evangelistic crusade in Kansas City. The whole visit was all very helpful and at the end of the three weeks I was clear in my own mind that I should accept their invitation rather than become a staff member at the EA.

On the subject of divine guidance. I had felt that it was a mistake to change direction too radically in response to God's call unless such a change became overwhelmingly apparent. This sequence of events seemed to be in direct answer to our prayer for God's guidance during this important period of our lives. As it happened I had written out a testimony, in response to a Billy Graham team member's request, so that Mr. Graham would know of the unusual sequence of events that led us to give our time to working with the 1966 Earls Court Crusade in Leicester. This account was not intended for wider publication but it was published in The Christian shortly after the Earls Court Crusade in June 1966 (See Chapter 28).

The choice of the Rev. George Hoffman as founder director of TEAR Fund was subsequently vindicated by the phenomenal growth of the fund. It grew from several thousand pounds to over ten million pounds per annum. Cliff Richard said, on more than one occasion, that TEAR Fund stopped him thinking about his personal needs and focused his thinking on the needs of others. Cliff has always been generous in his charitable giving - after his singing and filming assignments in Bangladesh and other underdeveloped countries, I think his involvement with TEAR Fund, of which he is Vice President, represents a substantial part of the Fund's annual income.

Whilst maintaining its original aims, TEAR Fund has now expanded its brief to include the award of development grants, support for evangelism and Christian education, the individual sponsorship of children and students in developing countries, handicraft marketing and the assignment of skilled personnel to about seventy overseas countries. For twenty-five years TEAR Fund has had a vital role as an agent for long term change. Working alongside local people, through development and training programmes, they are helping communities fight the underlying causes of poverty. In the slums of Delhi, in the shanty towns of Mexico, among the mountains of Nepal and along the plains of Africa, Christians are hard at work bringing the hope of the gospel, as well as health and harvest.

# Chapter 31 - Billy Graham: Personal Impressions

I will not attempt in this chapter to write the story of Billy Graham's life, as it has been fully chronicled in at least a score of biographies that have been published to date. You will need to read one or two of these biographies to discover how an obscure farm boy from the southern United States town of Charlotte, North Carolina became the world's best known preacher and at the same time the confidant of royalty, Presidents and leaders in every walk of life.

The published Billy Graham biographies range from John Pollock's authorised version to the one written by Marshall Frady, *A Parable of American Righteousness*. Both books have been published by Hodder and Stoughton. The first volume will intrigue and fascinate the evangelist's friends and supporters whilst the second will meet with the approval of his critics and opponents. These personal notes are not intended to be gossipy but I hope that they will provide the reader with insights into the less publicised aspects of Billy Graham's remarkable life and ministry.

His standard response, when introduced to someone is, "Please call me Billy".

During personal meetings with individuals he listened more than he talked and made everyone he met feel they were the most important person in the world.

Billy met Ruth while they were both students at theological college in the United States. She was the daughter of missionary parents in China. It would be impossible to overestimate the value that Ruth has been in his evangelistic ministry around the world. This was helped by a delightful sense of humour.

Ruth attended a Bible College in the United States in preparation for serving as a spinster missionary in Tibet. After Billy became famous, Ruth was frequently called on to address assemblies of Christian wives and mothers. As Frady recalls in his biography, Ruth told these women, "The best advice I've ever known is, your business is not to make your husband perfect but to make him happy. Study your husband, find out what kind of woman he needs. If you were a man, what kind of wife would you want to come home to? Don't disagree with your husband when he's absolutely bushed at night or when your hair is in curlers. "Graham himself was equally enthusiastic about his wife, "She has my cup of coffee right there every morning when I wake up. I've never seen her moody. She's always positive. She's always on the upbeat. I've never heard her say, "I'm tired" or "I'm depressed". I've never known her to lie down in the daytime. She just amazes me. She has no moods at all. She's wonderful. She's always the same!"

They brought up five children and Billy says of Ruth, "She rarely ever shows temperament. Her disposition is the same all the time - very sweet, very gracious, very charming and a great student of the Bible. Her life is ruled by the Bible more than any person I've ever known. That's her rule book, her compass."

Ruth had an unusual capacity for bringing up the five children, virtually alone, and her standard response was to say, "I'd rather have a little of Bill than a lot of any other man!"

Ruth Graham was a winsome speaker.... she was warmly appreciated when she frankly told a group of wives, "I find Christian parents without problem children can be stuffy. If you have a prodigal you will love all prodigals". Ruth knew only too well because all of their five children had their rebellious phases.

Ruth revealed to one journalist that when Billy was alone at home his favourite meal consisted of baked beans, Vienna sausages and canned tomatoes.

The Graham's lifestyle is quite frugal and far from extravagant. I remember the one occasion when we shared lunch together in their London hotel room. It consisted of a bowl of soup and a club sandwich.

Billy and Ruth Graham submitted to the security restrictions that their celebrity status demanded of them. When they started to receive letters that threatened Billy's life, security forces surrounded their mountainside home with an eight foot high fence and they were further protected by FBI trained guard dogs.

Billy never fails to pay tribute to the influence of his wife, Ruth, on his worldwide ministry. Even at the busiest times he always shows her the utmost courtesy. For instance, he invariably stands when she enters or leaves the room, even at times when he is in deep discussion with friends or colleagues.

He was initially converted at the age of 16 when he screwed up courage to attend a revival meeting in a tent that was pitched near his parents' farm in Charlotte, North Carolina. The evangelist was Mordecai Ham, who itinerated with his portable tabernacle which he erected on derelict street corners around the southern States of America. Ham took as his subject that evening, 'The Devils Big Three - Dances, Card Parties and Booze'. Young Billy could not relate to any of these temptations, having been brought up in a devout Christian home, but he raised his hand with other enquirers when the Kentucky evangelist invited a response. Billy's life was changed from that time onwards.

The work of YFC (Youth for Christ) began in Chicago at the end of the Second World War. The President of YFC, Dr. Torrey M. Johnson, recruited a team of four fellow evangelists to accompany him on a tour of the United Kingdom. They became known as the Boy Preachers and caused some amusement with their flamboyant ties, floppy black Bibles and dramatic preaching style. Billy Graham was a member of this team and shortly after returning home in 1947 he wrote the following to the editor of The Christian newspaper, ".....Our plane arrived at noon. Before I went to bed that night, I had three T-bone Steaks, about a gallon of milk, all the ice cream I could hold and all the other trimmings that went with it. Needless to say, I suffered from indigestion, but it was the best feeling of indigestion I had ever had!".

When Billy Graham came to Britain, to conduct his Harringay Crusade in 1954, he crossed the Atlantic in the Queen Mary. On board a hostile reporter posed a question that brought out the best in a team member who answered the question on Mr. Graham's behalf. The reporter asked, "Why, when Jesus had ridden into Jerusalem on an ass, did Billy Graham found it necessary to travel on a luxury liner". The reply was, "Well, brother, if you find us an ass that can swim the Atlantic, we'll be glad to try it".

The BGEA was a name which Billy Graham strenuously objected to when it was first suggested. It was formed in 1950 to launch his Hour of Decision radio programme. This was quickly followed by films and television broadcasts based on his crusading around the world. He also published the Decision magazine, books and a syndicated newspaper column, My Answer.

One of his closest associates said that, "Billy is a great delegator, trusting that you'll get on with the job without standing over your shoulder to monitor what you are doing". His colleague adds that, "he's a good forgiver when mistakes occur and is extraordinarily generous with praise towards those who work with him".

Billy Graham not only warned his team of associates against the temptations of pride, love of money and sexual involvement, he built in safeguards that helped team members avoid these specific pitfalls. His own personal Board of Directors took steps to ensure that the evangelist's own finances remained well within ethically defensible limits. His personal salary was limited to that of a minister of an average sized church and he refused to accept so called love-gifts. It was also one of his rules only to enter a hotel bedroom or lift if a team member was with him. The media in the United States were keen to find any evidence out of which they could create a scandal.

Billy Graham would use any innovation that promised to lengthen the reach or enhance the effectiveness of efforts to fulfil the Great Commission to preach the gospel to all nations.

The 1966 London Crusade began a new chapter in Billy Graham's ministry, in that it marked his first use of CCTV to carry crusade services to audiences far from the central arena. By using all the Eidophor projection equipment and post office land lines, available in Britain, electronic engineers were able to supply television feeds to ten cities at a time. One of the strengths of these satellite crusades was the way the image of the preacher on the huge screen allowed viewers freedom from the distracting echoes and the inevitable visual diversions, meaning they were able to concentrate on the message of the evangelist.

The basic affirmation of his sermons during the fifty years of crusading never varied from the declaration that, "Jesus died so that sinners might be forgiven, have their lives transformed and find peace with God".

When Billy was asked how he felt while he was making the appeal for people to make a public commitment to Christ, he said that it always took a great deal out of him. His reply to this question was, "In the few minutes after I call people to Christ, when I'm standing there not saying a word, that's when my strength leaves me. I don't usually get tired quickly, but I get exhausted in those moments. I don't know what it is, but something is going out at that moment".

In the 1970's he gave much more emphasis, in his preaching, to a growing awareness of social unrest and the needs of the poor and hungry peoples of the world. He told students, "As a Christian, I believe that God has a special concern for things like peace, racism, the responsible use of Earth's resources, economic and social justice, the use of power and the sacredness of human life".

Many journalists consider Billy Graham to be a unique figure in the history of evangelism. It is true, of course, that he had the advantages of amplification, telecommunication and satellite broadcasting, but there had been notable mass evangelists in earlier centuries. For instance, the 18th Century evangelist, George Whitefield preached unaided to crowds of 20,000 who flocked to his open air rallies. In the last quarter of the 19th Century the American preacher, Dwight L. Moody electrified 9,000 people who came to listen to him during each day of his London campaign. In 1954 Billy Graham packed an indoor stadium, at Harringay Arena, with crowds of 12,000 a night for an unbroken period of 3 months and climaxed it with a service in Wembley Stadium which attracted congregations of 60,000 and 120,000. Police estimate that over two million heard him preach in person in the centre of the South Korean capital, Seoul, in the late 1960's.

He came, on a memorable occasion, to speak to the hundred or so evangelists who were attending their annual gathering at a Conference Centre in southern England. He told the group of aspiring evangelists, "We need to preach with compassion. People should sense that you love them, that you are interested in them. Even when you preach about Hell", Graham continued, "You need to convey that God speaks from a broken heart".

Music Guests Johnny Cash, Cliff Richard, Ethyl Walters, Bev Shea, George Hamilton IV and a host of other Country & Western singers made notable contributions at Billy Graham's crusades. During the years I got to know these musicians, there is no doubting their integrity in accepting Mr. Graham's invitation to contribute during the crusade services.

A Texan oil billionaire made an offer of six million dollars for him to run for the presidency in 1952 on a Back to God ticket. Billy Graham is reported to have given the idea, 'earnest and prayerful consideration'. When he told Ruth about the proposal she is reported to have told him that she did not think the American people would vote for a divorced president, and if he left the ministry for politics he would certainly have a divorce on his hands.

Apart from his understandable early faux pas with President Harry Truman, Billy was resolutely discreet over his conversations with the famous. He met the most formidable figures of the second half of the twentieth century - Queen Elizabeth (with whom he dined on a number of occasions), Winston Churchill, Golda Meir, Indira Gandhi and King Hussein.

It has to be admitted that Billy Graham acted in a rather politically naive way on occasions. For instance, he allowed most of the Presidential candidates to speak from his crusade platform immediately prior to their candidacy for President of the United States. He always claimed that he was neutral politically and refused to support any of the candidates but, of course, their appearances gave the impression that he was publicly endorsing their candidacy. Billy Graham has attended and been involved in the inaugurations of Presidents Clinton, Bush, Reagan, Nixon, Johnson and Eisenhower.

I suppose Billy had imperfections but for a man who was in the spotlight, his integrity and motives were never questioned. During his long 40 year ministry, Billy Graham has suffered from a long list of illnesses. Even his closest associates admit that he is something of a hypochondriac. While he has, like most evangelists, an ego, he is a genuinely humble man. Paradoxically he yearns for privacy but feels hurt if people do not recognise him. He tells interviewers about his accomplishments but doubts whether they will really count for much to future historians.

He was skilled in answering questions at press conferences on a wide range of topics. Having attended a number of these I never knew him to be rude or impatient with reporter's questions, however unreasonable. He was frequently criticised on these occasions for incurring unnecessary expense, psychological manipulation of the crowds, his association with President Nixon, his support of the war in Vietnam, his co-operation with non-evangelicals and his opposition to communism.

He was asked about teetotalism. Graham told reporters that he, "sometimes had a sip of wine before going to bed", adding that Jesus turned water into real wine at a wedding feast.

Billy Graham was not only criticised and misreported by the Press, he suffered the same treatment at the hands of his more fundamentalist brethren in the United States. He told one radio audience, "By God's grace I will make it a policy never to answer critics.... I shall continue to preach the Gospel of Jesus Christ and not stoop to mudslinging, name-calling and petty little fights over non-essentials".

In one of his televised appearances with David Frost, Billy Graham lost a substantial number of his traditional supporters when he answered the interviewer's question, "Who do you think is the most important religious leader of the twentieth century?". He replied, "I would think that would be possibly Pope John. I think that he opened a gigantic Pandora's Box within the Church of Rome that has affected the whole of the world church. I'm not a historian enough, or theologian enough, to know exactly where it's going to take us or fully what's happening, but something of major proportions, a revolution within the church is taking place.....".

Billy was invited to be the speaker at the centenary service for the annual Keswick Convention. He and the other team members travelled from London to Keswick by train and en route they had lunch in the restaurant car. After taking his order the waitress asked Billy if he would like anything to drink. He ordered cider for himself. This must have greatly surprised her because she exclaimed, "If you hadn't ordered that glass of cider I would have sworn that you were Billy Graham". This response apparently amused Billy who told her that Christians were free to enjoy all of God's gifts. When he arrived at Keswick, Billy Graham found that the organising committee had arranged for him to travel across the lake on a launch to the shoreside where fifteen thousand had assembled for the special centenary service.

Another notable event to which Billy was invited as a special speaker was the 350th anniversary of the sailing of the Pilgrim Fathers to America. The Royal Albert Hall was booked for the event and a luxury commemorative programme, under the title Freedom and Faith, was printed on parchment paper and given to the eight thousand guests who attended the meeting. The occasion took the form of a pageant that told the story of the voyage of the Pilgrim Fathers from England to America. A Grenadier Guards band accompanied the pageant. Following the special anniversary meeting in the Albert Hall, Billy Graham spoke to two hundred VIP's from all walks of life who had responded to his invitation to dinner at the Hyde Park Hotel. A team member was allocated to each table of celebrities. I remember the tennis player, Virginia Wade, and the film star, Thora Hird, were at the table where Mary and I were sitting. The dinner was, of course, a formal occasion and having collected my evening suit from Moss Bros. I was embarrassed to find that a pair of cuff links was not included with the white dress shirt. All of this was forgotten once Billy Graham began his address, which seemed to be well received by those present.

# Chapter 32 - Billy's Team

The greatest privilege, to those invited by Billy Graham to become an associate, was the opportunity to attend the bi-annual team meeting. This was usually held at one of the leading hotels in the United States. This facility was paid for by businessmen who supported Mr. Graham's worldwide ministry.

Mary and I attended our first team meeting at the Greenbrier Hotel, White Sulphur Springs in the State of Virginia. It provided the most luxurious accommodation imaginable with its own championship golf course. We were surprised to discover that the team consisted of no fewer than 150 members. It included such personal guests of Billy Graham as a couple of bishops, several prominent theologians and two or three political leaders.

Billy and Ruth were the gracious hosts of the five-day gathering and although Billy was tired he gave two vigorous addresses to the team, mainly to encourage. He showed a very genuine concern for each member of the team and I remember one particular address when he made an impassioned plea for us all to live a more sanctified lifestyle. He warned against three specific temptations which he said were inherent in an itinerant evangelistic calling i.e. the love of money, pride and sexual compromise. His eyes filled with tears as he recalled the backsliding of a couple of earlier associates, who had failed in these areas of their lives. This was, of course, many years before the world was shocked by the scandalous behaviour of the so called tele-evangelists.

The team meeting was meant for rest and mutual encouragement. As is well known, Billy along with his immediate associates, friends and boyhood chums, T.W. Wilson and Grady

Wilson, relaxed during a round of golf together. For me the greatest benefit in attending the meeting was to get acquainted with some of the men and women who were household names in the world of evangelism.

Perhaps the one who influenced me the most was Dr. J. Edwin Orr. His books on the Awakenings in Britain and the United States gave an accurate account of how God's Spirit sparked revival and the beginnings of such missionary movements as the China Inland Mission and the Salvation Army. Billy Graham believed that Edwin Orr was instrumental in mobilising the prayer support that led to the spiritual breakthrough of his evangelistic ministry at the Los Angeles Crusade in 1948.

Billy Graham also invited Dr. Orr to give lectures, to the School of Evangelism, that were sponsored by a Texan millionaire for the benefit of theological students and others accepting the invitation to attend during each of the major Graham crusades. Edwin Orr traced the history of the great evangelical revivals of the eighteenth century in order to raise a sense of expectation that the Lord could do it all over again in answer to repentance and prayer. Dr. Orr stressed that renewal amongst the people of God was a necessary prerequisite to revival in the wider community. He said that, in his experience, the period of intensive preparation that surrounded an area-wide crusade provided the conditions which brought about renewal within churches who participated in the crusade.

During the afternoons, when other team members were on the golf course or sleeping off the hotel's lavish meals, I usually found Edwin Orr in the corner of a lounge on his own and eager for conversation. I had already read and been fascinated by some of his twenty books, in which he described leaving his home in Ireland as a teenager and arriving in Liverpool with an old bicycle and two shillings and eightpence farthing in cash. His first book, *Can God?* was one of half a dozen chronicles that record the 'ten thousand miles of miracles in Britain' which he saw in those first two years away from home. Edwin responded keenly to my questioning regarding the basis on which the Holy Spirit poured out an awakening on a community. He said that provided God's work was done in God's way and in God's time, He invariably honoured it with a mighty outpouring of His Spirit.

Dr. Edwin Orr organised annual lectures on 'revival' at Oxford University. During one of these evenings he asked if I could record interviews with him, which could then be transcribed for publication in one of his forthcoming volumes. As a direct outcome of these interviews he introduced me to several of the major Christian publishers in the United States including Zondervan and Doubleday.

On Dr. Orr's recommendation these publishers commissioned me to record interviews with the major authors on their book list. These included Corrie Ten Boom, Jim Packer, John Stott, Helen Roseveare, Stephen Olford, Joni Erickson and Jackie Pullinger. These publishers paid what, at that time, seemed a magnificent fee of 250 dollars per interview plus travel and accommodation expenses. The cassettes of these recorded interviews were distributed through the book trade and Christian press in the United States and the rest of the English speaking world to promote the sale of the interviewees' books. As I retained the copyright on the interviews, I submitted selected ones to the BBC and several were accepted for broadcast in BBC programming at home and overseas.

As you will gather, my contacts with Dr. Edwin Orr were exceedingly helpful to building up confidence in the next stages of my work. During the course of the years Edwin established hundreds of Revival groups around the world and he passed on to each Hudson Taylor's motto, "There is a living God: He has spoken in the Bible, He means what He says and will do all that He promised".

I was once asked what qualified me as an interviewer. I think, to be honest, I have an innate curiosity about people and a desire to know more of the person behind the mask that well known individuals tend to erect to conceal their own true personalities. A good interviewer is also one who can express enthusiasm about subjects on which he is far from fanatical. The fifteen minute interview format, usually requested by the publishers, allowed for a fairly in-depth biographical sketch of each interviewee plus a brief synopsis of the book under review. I was quite happy to undertake not to edit out any significant part of the interview that could alter the sense of the whole. At the same time I tried to avoid the bland kind of exchange that allowed for the evasion of probing questions.

Christian authors can be every bit as evasive as politicians and both need to be pressed to reveal their true feelings on their chosen subjects. In the case of people for whom one had a tremendous respect, I found it necessary to keep my nerve and even, at times, to ask what may have appeared an unsympathetic or surprise question. I believe that the interviewer has a responsibility to ask the question that the listener wants to hear answered. I made a habit of never indicating in advance but sought simply to obtain information on behalf of the listener. I only remember getting into difficulty for this reason on two occasions. To give one example - I asked a high profile American Christian Aid executive to justify the lavish lifestyle that he led while travelling through developing countries. He took offence at this line of questioning and sadly the publisher edited out this revealing exchange before the cassettes were distributed.

# Chapter 33 - Stages in a Billy Graham Crusade

During the late 1960's, when I joined Billy Graham's team, the evangelist was actively considering a short list of twenty or thirty invitations for crusades during the next five years.

The majority of invitations he received to conduct a crusade did not meet the criteria which, he and his senior associates felt, satisfied the minimum conditions that were necessary for further discussion and prayer. The delays inevitably involved in this process proved to be frustrating to those who had initiated these invitations. Over the years, however, Billy had learned to judge which city was likely to attract the maximum prayer and preparation for a united evangelistic endeavour on such a scale that the entire community would hear his message.

Unless there was a particularly urgent reason for Billy to accept an invitation at short notice, such as happened in the southern United States at a time of racial disharmony, Billy would arrange for one of his preparatory men to visit the cities on the short list every few months. If and when Mr. Graham provisionally accepted an invitation, a preparatory man was appointed by him as his Crusade Director for that specific campaign and he would visit the city every few weeks. The nominee Crusade Director was then responsible for advising Billy Graham on the potential prayer and financial support that could be expected in the area concerned. The Crusade Director's responsibility was also to sound out the local churches and lay leaders in the community. If they proved to be acceptable Billy would write a personally signed letter saying how much he was depending on their co-operation.

I should refer at this stage to a remarkable man that I met at one of Billy's team meetings. He was quite an eccentric and had the unusual name of Willis Haymaker. Billy had taken him on as a team member for the purpose of visiting the more sacrificial donors. Over a meal Willis, who was in his mid-90's, told me that he enjoyed this work. It involved him in visiting donors, unannounced, to bring Billy's greetings personally and to thank them on his behalf for supporting his ministry in such practical ways with their financial gifts. (I also discovered that Willis was Billy Sunday's Crusade Director. Billy Sunday was a sort-of Billy Graham in the second half of the 19th Century. I mention this because Mr. Graham adopted many of Sunday's crusade procedures in the later preparatory stages for his own meetings.)

Two or three days before Billy Graham was due to preach at the first crusade service he gave an address for crusade workers. He would arrive at the location and begin with a visit to the crusade office. There he sought to express appreciation to all the volunteer workers. Some of these had worked for over a year in sending out prayer bulletins for the area-wide crusade, recruiting attendance at prayer groups and classes for those who wished to be involved in counselling people who came forward at the evangelistic invitation.

During these two or three days, Billy also visited the auditorium where the crusade meetings were to be held and spoke at a meeting for the Crusade Executive Committee and other church leaders in the area covered by the crusade.

On the morning of the crusade itself Mr. Graham addressed a Press Conference, which he did with consummate skill, and answered questions from the press representatives who were present.

# PART 7 - RADIO

John Interviewing

# Chapter 34 - Our Children's Education

In the autumn of 1967 we moved away from Leicester in search of a fresh start. I managed to arrange a £7,500 mortgage and we were soon moving to a detached house with a large garden in a small village called South Nutfield, which nestles below the North Downs in Surrey. The house, known as 'Dawn Cottage', became the family home for over twenty years and was a perfect place for the children to grow up.

Our three children, Robert, Alastair and Christine were a constant source of joy and, occasionally, heartache to us. I will not intrude on their privacy again, but these pages fill in the gaps between their infancy and the time they left home.

During his childhood, Robert enjoyed the company of a mythical family. He called them The Bullers and he not only talked about them but to them. Somehow, he seemed to need these unseen companions to whom he could confide his intimate thoughts. Robert was public spirited from a young age. He and a couple of friends held occasional sales of their toys, books and clothes in our garage. They gave the money raised from the sales to the RSPCA and other charities.

Robert won a scholarship to Reigate Grammar School. Shortly after his 12th birthday in October 1967, he began publishing the *Library Times* which he described as the 'Magazine of South Nutfield Library'. It was a bi-monthly publication which he laboriously wrote by hand and then distributed it to about a dozen subscribers. The Library, which he kept on shelves and in boxes in his bedroom, consisted of books which he bought second-hand and supplemented by those titles given to him by family and friends.

The *Library Times*, with its review of new additions to the Library, continued for twenty-five editions.

At the end of 1970 Robert launched his bi-monthly *Crusader Comet*. He was, at the time, an enthusiastic member of the local Crusader Group - a national, inter-denominational Christian movement for teenage boys. The first edition of the *Crusader Comet* consisted of twelve duplicated pages and cost 2.5 pence a copy. The initial print run of 40 copies sold out. True to its title it became quite a crusading magazine and before it folded after two and a half years, in March 1973, it contained controversial but well researched articles. These offered Crusader members a Christian perspective on say, Apartheid in South Africa and Nuclear Disarmament. During his early years in the Crusader class Robert was zealous in sharing his Christian faith with school friends and others.

In his final year at Reigate Grammar School, Robert made a significant advance up the literary ladder. He was invited to take responsibility for editing his school magazine, *The Pilgrim*. This was a prestigious, litho-printed, quarterly publication. It was not in Robert's nature to boast about his appointment but it was an appropriate recognition for getting top marks in his last but one English Literature examination. Some of Robert's sixth form contemporaries became school Prefects but his housemaster probably felt that our son would be more comfortable making a literary contribution. Robert not only enjoyed editing *The Pilgrim* but also wrote thoughtful editorials, short stories and reports on Reigate Grammar Schools' sporting activities.

During the summer holidays Robert joined a group of volunteers, from his Crusader group, working on the picturesque Ffestiniog steam railway in North Wales. The narrow gauge railway was originally constructed to carry slate mined from the quarries between Portmaddock and Ffestiniog. Unpaid working parties have been regularly recruited for years to carry out maintenance tasks on the tracks, embankments, bridges and stations. The volunteers came from all age groups and lived in Youth Hostels near to the railway. The old steam locomotives are mostly driven by retired British Rail drivers. The engines haul lovingly refurbished carriages. These are filled during the holiday months with tourists and at all times of the year by steam enthusiasts, who travel on the train in a nostalgic bid to recapture the memories of a bygone age.

When he left Reigate Grammar School, Robert worked on the staff of a leading private bank in the City of London and at an American bank in Germany. In his mid-twenties he led quite an adventurous, back-packing life in several Mediterranean and Far Eastern countries. Robert returned home physically drained and emotionally shattered after escaping out of one or two tight corners.

Charles Alastair, who was two years younger than Robert John, was quite different from his older brother temperamentally. Alastair was less of an activist and sports enthusiast than Robert. This was partly because he developed asthma when he was less than a year old. He communicated his thoughts through poetry rather than prose. While he was still at Junior School Alastair became a subscribing member of the RSPCA and he signed a pledge, 'to be kind to animals and birds and to do my best to protect them from cruel treatment'.

While he was a student at the local Technical College Alastair was influenced by the spiritual renewal movement, popularly known as the Jesus People. The movement, which featured as a cover story in TIME magazine, swept like a prairie fire through the United States and across the Atlantic to Britain. In common with other revolutionary movements it attracted to its fringes numerous counterfeits and charlatans. More importantly, however, the message and socially aware music of the Jesus People had a radical impact on the lifestyle and discipleship of disaffected young Christians. They were literally practising the Sermon on the Mount.

The influence of the movement also challenged the materialistic philosophy and hedonistic culture of the affluent West. Not surprisingly it also disturbed the lethargy of some of the moribund churches, which had failed to give relevant answers to the questions countless drug addicts and dropouts were asking. The teaching and example that the radical Jesus People offered to thousands in the hippy, flower power generation of the 60's gave them a new purpose for living. Some of the more institutionalised churches found it difficult to accommodate this 'new wine' in their old 'wine skins'. Those who did welcome these new Christians were immeasurably, if at times painfully, enriched by a fresh infusion of spiritual life.

Alastair made no attempt to conceal his involvement in this dynamic new Christian force. A variety of Jesus Stickers appeared on his clothes and covered his well-thumbed and heavily notated Living Bible. He attended, with other youngsters from his church, large rallies at which the American cross carrying street evangelist, Arthur Blessitt, gave his dramatic testimony. Musicians such as Larry Norman and The Fisherfolk were notable exponents of the Jesus People. I still have a tape recording of Alastair talking about his new experiences. He grew in confidence and handed out tracts to friends at school. However, the inward change was reflected by the caring attitude which he showed to others in need.

After qualifying at Redhill Technical College, for university entrance, Alastair spent the first year working as a male nurse at a large mental hospital in Surrey. Despite the attempts to humanise the institution it remained a grim Victorian lunatic asylum. Discipline was still enforced by a strict regime of drugs, padded rooms, secure wards and physical force. The nursing staff were discouraged from developing personal relationships with individual patients but Alastair was often upset by the rough treatment meted out to patients who failed to conform to the strict hospital regime. Alastair also mediated in the case of some of the patients in his care, who were the subjects of cruelty and injustice. He resumed his duties at the hospital during his holidays from University. I like Alastair. In fact I have grown to enjoy all our children but I feel completely at ease with him.

Alastair studied for three years at Stirling University in Scotland. He read for and obtained a B.Sc. degree in Psychology. The course subjects included biology, sociology and psychology. He wrote a thesis on graphology, which is the study of handwriting. Some employers and recruitment agencies claim that handwriting provides a reliable character assessment of individual candidates.

Christine was born three months after Alastair's third birthday. We gave her our three favourite girl's names - Christine, Elizabeth and Mary. I was especially delighted to welcome a little girl into our family at last. In common with other enterprising children, Christine's life was a series of ups and downs. I can remember, for instance, how much she had been looking forward to the arrival of Ruth and made no secret of her disappointment when her baby sister failed to arrive. It did not make much sense to her to be told that Ruth had gone straight to be with Jesus. It became apparent quite early on that she was left handed which made some of her school work difficult.

When Christine was just three years old we left the Exclusive Brethren. She was an intelligent child and nothing we did could shield her from the trauma of being expelled from the company of all our family and friends. She was a great favourite with her grandparents, aunts and uncles. No one could assess the confusion that she and her brothers suffered through the enforced separation from other family members. We were later greatly relieved to find that the children had suffered no lasting psychological damage from all the emotional turmoil that had been forced on our family life.

Christine had struggled with academic subjects at school from an early age. It was only when she attended Redhill Technical College, however, that a recently diagnosed condition known as dyslexia was suggested. Dyslexia is a form of word blindness which may be caused by a neurological disorder. One effect of the condition prevents sufferers from getting their thoughts into writing.

At 17, she took a residential job with Community Service Volunteers as a Care Assistant at a centre for young people in Liverpool. Not surprisingly Christine grew attached to the physically and mentally handicapped teenagers living in the community home to which she was assigned. As some of these youngsters were deprived of love and appreciation they responded to hers in full measure. I spent one weekend as a guest of the community home and it was one of the most enjoyable weekends of my life.

Previously, she had been involved in befriending teenagers who were making frequent appearances in the magistrates' court and serving probationary terms for petty offences. For one period of several months she lived in a well-disciplined hippy commune. Hers was a roller-coaster of a life.

Christine then began her career as an apprentice carpenter and joiner with a local firm. At the same time she was doing her City and Guilds course. She achieved a Distinction for this, designing and making some exquisite pieces of furniture which included a roll top desk and a drawing room cupboard. Following this she spent a year at the London College of Furniture.

At the age of 25 Christine packed up her tools and set off for Toledo Technical College in Belize, Central America. She went for two years to teach carpentry to youngsters between the ages of 15 and 21. All of her practical experience led her to believe that she should offer herself for a term of service with Voluntary Service Overseas.

# Chapter 35 - Journalism and Interview

## JOURNALISM

When asked how I became involved in journalism I regret that my answer is less than helpful. This is because so many of the earliest opportunities I had for reporting events and interviewing those involved in them depended on my association with Billy Graham.

In common with other members of the evangelists' team, we were often invited to appear on local television and radio stations and be written about in the local press. On balance, however, I much preferred to be on the other side of the microphone where my natural curiosity about people was given greater scope. In my day there were no minimum educational requirements or degrees awarded to examination candidates before they were accredited as journalists. Most of my younger colleagues served their apprenticeships in journalism by making routine visits to local sources of news, such as police stations, hospitals and town halls. Today, however, most universities provide candidates with a degree course in media studies and, in my opinion, more creative writers are prevented from entering the profession because of the need for these academic credentials.

Members of the Arts Centre Group, who were engaged in journalism of one sort or another, often debated whether a radio station or newspaper would increase its listeners, viewers or readers if it devoted its entire news output to good news.

We agreed, of course, that as Christians we had a duty to reflect the spectrum of changes that are changing our world and all assumed that our material would be both accurate and fair. There was a time when I was in favour of always finding room for an 'and finally.....' tailpiece (just a funny or light-hearted story) so as to leave the readers or listeners with a smile. Now I prefer the reported comment of the BBC's Director General, John Birt, who told his staff that the BBC should think in terms of providing nourishment for the young, vulnerable and deprived, ".....by helping them to find ways to deal with their problems, by raising their aspirations, by exposing them to influences that would enhance and not reduce their lives".

In the world of international journalism, 'good news' stories are few and far between and when they do occur these tend to be given low priority by the news editor. This is because he is looking for stories that feature conflict, death or disaster and so, unfortunately, the greater the tragedy the more prominence it gains.

Before the reader turns another page, I would like to acknowledge my indebtedness to four distinguished media-men who were quite selfless in sharing with me not only their time but their skills. It was through their influence that I was drawn somehow into the world of journalism and broadcasting which would provide me with a fresh turning point in my career. The four are:

Malcom Muggeridge, the renowned satirist and newspaper columnist,

Wynford Vaughan-Thomas, the Welsh writer and broadcaster,

James D. Douglas, who edited three of the standard Christian dictionaries to be published in the twentieth century, and

Gerald Priestland, when he was the BBC's religious affairs correspondent.

By the time Malcom Muggeridge reached his old age he was satirised as 'Saint Mug'. In his youth, however, he was an advocate of the permissive society and militant atheism. By the end of his illustrious career, which included several years when he edited Punch Magazine, he became one of the sternest critics of the sexual immorality and materialism that characterised the 1960's. His pilgrimage from agnosticism to Christianity made front page news in the 1970's when he announced his resignation as the Rector of Edinburgh University. The news of this climaxed the speech in which he had denounced the taking of 'pills and pot' by students at the University. After his resignation Muggeridge was shunned by members of the intellectual establishment.

I first encountered Malcom Muggeridge when I took on the task of interviewing five individuals at a massive open air rally in Trafalgar Square in the mid-70's. The rally was co-ordinated by the NFOL (Nationwide Festival of Light), which was led at that time by Mrs. Mary Whitehouse. The rally marked a moral renaissance on the part of several religious, political and social groups. Each had taken a distinctive stand on family values, peace initiatives and human rights. They formed a coalition which drew together and gave voice to 20,000 who attended the initial rally in Central London on that Saturday afternoon.

My first interviewee represented the women's peace movement in Northern Ireland, another had banned pornographic material from his newsagents shop and at least one spoke against the alleged injustice caused by the imposition of closed shop membership in the Trade Union in which he had been involved for many years. I was only allocated 3 or 4 minutes for each of these interviews. This was difficult enough without the distractions that were present in Trafalgar Square.

As I climbed the platform between the two lions, I spotted Mr. Muggeridge sitting with the other front row of guests who were facing the speakers at the microphone. He was renowned at that time for his weekly in-depth television interviews with celebrities who were involved in current affairs. In spite of the difficulties I conducted the series of interviews to the best of my ability, but left the platform feeling that neither my guests nor I felt satisfied with our contribution to the rally. After descending from the platform I felt a firm hand on my shoulder and looking behind me I was surprised to see the face of Malcom Muggeridge. He greatly encouraged me with the words, "Well done, my boy, I couldn't have done better myself". From then on he urged me from time to time to keep on writing and interviewing.

It was not always easy to get Malcom Muggeridge to testify to his Christian experience but at one press conference he expressed it in these elegant words,

"There was no point in my life when I underwent a dramatic change. The process has not been a sudden Damascus road experience, but more like the journeying of Bunyan's Pilgrim, who constantly lost his way, fell into sloughs, was locked up in Doubting Castle and was terrified out of his wits in the Valley of the Shadow of Death, but still through it all I had a sense of moving towards light and of moving out of time towards eternity. That's the most that I can claim."

I have quoted his daily prayer later in the book but it is worth repeating it here;

"O God, stay with me, let no word cross my lips that is not Your word, no thought enter my mind that is not Your thought, no deed ever be done or entertained by me that is not Your deed."

During the years when I worked in Christian radio I had the opportunity of meeting a number of people who became well known in the media at large. The following are extracts from interviews I did with some of these well-known individuals:

Perhaps the most impressive person that I ever met was Mother Teresa of Calcutta, who was awarded the Nobel Peace Prize for her work of caring for the destitute and dying around the world. Mother Teresa perfectly emphasised the words of St. Francis to his followers eight hundred years ago. He told them, "Go into all the world and proclaim the Gospel, use words if you have to." After opening a new home in London for her Sisters of Charity she told me, "If we will give ourselves fully to God He will use us to do great things for Him, on condition that we believe much more in His love than in our own weakness."

I had the opportunity of meeting and interviewing Mr. Wynford Vaughan-Thomas during the Billy Graham Crusade in 1967. He was a guest speaker at one of the services held in Earls Court. After leaving the BBC as its senior Welsh staff member he set up a private closed circuit television company. He did this by buying up all of the Eidophor closed circuit television projectors that had been made by Phillips, the only manufacturer of these specialist projectors.

As a youth Wynford went to the same Swansea school as Dylan Thomas and for some years he was the drinking companion of the renowned Welsh poet. Coming down from Oxford at the height of the Depression of the 1930's he struggled to earn a living as a lecturer in a night school for unemployed Welsh miners. Eventually he joined the BBC before the end of the war and as a BBC war correspondent he recorded, in the air, his impressions of an RAF raid on Berlin. Wynford told me how he was given the scripts of Winston Churchill's speeches when he gave the commentary at several of the great man's public functions. These were typed on easy-to-handle cards. Each manuscript was carefully orchestrated, with every pause marked and the words to be emphasised were underlined. After the war he broadcast many eye-witness events such as the Royal Tours of Commonwealth Countries and the handover of power in India.

Wynford vividly recalled the meeting he had with Mahatma Gandhi at one of his prayer durbars in Delhi. This was one of Gandhi's regular prayer meetings which he held on the lawn of his New Delhi home before he was assassinated. He recalled the 'frail, dark, emaciated figure who was wearing dark glasses and leaning on one of his disciples' and said that he felt the strange compelling power of the Indian leader.

Bishop Festo Kivengere of Uganda became a Christian as a schoolboy. He was one of the outstanding results of what has become known as the East African Revival. He was a close friend of Archbishop Janani Lowum who was martyred on the direct order of President Idi Amin and was with him just moments before he was taken away and shot by members of Amin's security forces. Bishop Kivengere escaped from Uganda but when his own life was threatened by Amin's administration he subsequently lived in Britain, in exile, for several years.

Unusually for a bishop he was better known for his evangelistic gifts and when we met in London I asked him how he would define the role of a bishop in the Anglican Church. He replied, "The Bishop is a shepherd and he is primarily an evangelist and a shepherd of the flock. One who shares the Word, one who actually protects the faith through the scriptures, expounding the Word of God, sharing his faith with his flock, encouraging his ministers with him as brothers in Christ. This is what the Bishop is all about. Then of course, in addition to that, he has administrative responsibilities too."

I commented, "You must be under tremendous pressure, with these onerous responsibilities, travelling all over the world speaking at large gatherings."

He answered, "Oh, pressures are there when you've got eight hundred and fifty churches over which you exercise a role as a Bishop and are responsible for a quarter of a million Christians with about fifty or sixty pastors. Now that is a big job in itself but I take it that when God wants you to minister He will always give you that extra. So instead of feeling the usual strain and almost killing yourself in order that you may fulfil the calling - I knew I couldn't do it. So what I did was to keep handing it over to the Lord and saying to Him that, "I can't do it, You do it for me. Work through my fumblings, my shortcomings, my failings and achieve Your purpose." And He did it beautifully. As to the travelling ministry, I have sometimes spoken without His permission and got very dry. I have had to repent of speaking without His permission and this of course keeps me fresh. In order to keep fresh in the ministry one has to learn the art of going back to the cross to repent of the sin of disobedience."

Dutch author and heroine Corrie Ten Boom never tired of recalling the adventures of her life in Holland during the German occupation and in the Ravensbruek concentration camp. She told me her story of how God 'shed abroad' His love in her heart, enabling her to forget her own misery and to care for her companions who, like her, were being persecuted by German guards. With God's help she was able, in time, to forgive the prison guards who tortured her.

Corrie Ten Boom's story of her suffering through brutality is told in the book and film, *The Hiding Place*. She lived well into her eighties and right until the end was still talking about the purpose of God in her suffering in Nazi concentration camps. She described her experience in this way, "Picture a piece of embroidery placed between you and God with the right side up towards God." She explained that during this life we can only see the loose frayed ends but God alone sees the completed pattern.

United States astronaut Colonel James Irwin held a press conference in a London hotel. He showed us a piece of moon rock, enclosed in a sort of old-fashioned glass cake dish, which he brought back from his walk on the Appenine Mountains of the moon. In a later interview he told me what it was like to take his first steps on the moon. He said, "I felt very special when I looked down at my footprints in the moon dust because the scientists on our Apollo 15 Mission said that they would be there for a million years". Colonel Irwin also recalled looking up and, "seeing the earth the size of a marble". He said, "It was beautiful and so far away and yet I felt strangely at home on the moon". The ex-astronaut concluded that prayer was very special to him because he felt its power and God's presence in a very special way on the moon. Colonel James Irwin was the eighth man to walk on the moon.

Translator of *The Living Bible*, Dr. Kenneth Taylor, began his task of paraphrasing the New Testament epistles so that his children could understand them during their evening bible study at home. He had no thought of publishing these paraphrases but during his daily train journey to work he set about translating the remainder of the New Testament and also the books of the Old Testament. He objected to my describing him as a Bible Translator saying that he was merely giving a thought for thought paraphrase from the original Greek and Hebrew into colloquial English. When I asked Dr. Taylor if he could give a couple of scripture verses for which he had no human responsibility he thought for a couple of minutes and then quoted the following;

Proverbs 3 v 5 & 6. ..... *trust the Lord completely; don't ever trust yourself. In everything you do, put God first, and he will direct you and crown your efforts with success.*

2 Corinthians 12 v 9. *Each time He said, "No. But I am with you; that is all you need. My power shows up best in weak people."*

# Chapter 36 - Broadcasting from Seychelles

The next four chapters were compiled from John's diary notes and letters that he wrote home.

John spent 4 five month stints working for FEBA (Far East Broadcasting Association) Radio in the Seychelles. The first two are covered in this chapter and are based on letters he sent home, a prayer newsletter and various diary notes. The following three chapters detail other assignments for FEBA Radio to India, again the Seychelles and finally, Africa.

FEBA Radio is broadcast to the Indian sub-continent and East Africa. These broadcasts are aimed at spreading the Christian Gospel but, as a way of increasing their audience, they also have an International News Service. Finding Christian missionaries with the skills and interest to provide such a service is not easy. John's initial placement was a temporary one until somebody else could be found. He started as a Newsroom trainee in his early fifties and soon graduated to becoming duty editor.

### Thursday 28th May 1981

*I haven't been able to write before because there is only one direct plane to England each week and that's on a Friday. Seychelles is quite beautiful - with the sea every shade of blue and lots of palm trees and a great variety of birds. I haven't felt the heat too much and only a couple of bites so far. Folks here have been so kind - a big box of grocery waiting in my flat on arrival last Saturday p.m. and I have been out to different families for lunch and dinner every day since. I start work proper next Sunday the 31st with the 5.30 a.m. shift, i.e. Monday and Wednesday off first week.*

We provide separate news programmes for South Asia and East Africa. So far I have been reading and listening to a great deal about these parts of our target area. I expect to be reading the news bulletins in about four to six weeks' time, after voice training has slowed me down, but up to then I will be compiling material from the various teleprinters and agency reports that come to the Newsroom.

The shops in Victoria are fascinating - lots of fish and fruit; local tea and coffee but bread and potatoes in short supply. In time I am getting used to the night sounds and sights - dogs barking; minah birds and crickets plus various kinds of insects roaming the house.

Thursday 4th June 1981

Love and greetings from sunny Seychelles. On Sunday, Tuesday and Thursday I started work in the Newsroom at 5.30 a.m. and finished at about 7.30 p.m. The intervening days have been officially off-duty and I spent one day on the beach and shopping, but on the remaining days I have been doing some voice training. Because English is the second language for many of our listeners in Africa and India, the pace needs to be much slower than my normal speech and my teacher thinks that I am making good progress to that end.

A day in the Newsroom is really hard but very interesting work. We make up two five-minute and two ten-minute bulletins each day from three News Agency teleprinters, plus news programmes broadcast by All India Radio, Radio Sri Lanka, BBC World Service, Swiss Radio and other international stations that we can pick up in the Seychelles. At present I work with colleagues and I don't expect to be given sole charge of the Newsroom for a few weeks yet - the news service has gained a good reputation for accuracy and I need to assimilate more background information about the target areas.

Things that I enjoy here are fresh lime juice (limes from the market are put through the liquidiser); tuna fish (freshly caught and cooked in the oven as a steak); the tremendous variety of bird life and the brilliant blue of the sea (with the coral below the surface). I'm also getting less jumpy about the insects that abound, although I do take exception to cockroaches that wander into my flat.

### Thursday 13th May 1982

It's difficult to believe that I've been here again for two weeks but I suppose the one-day-on, one-day-off rota makes time pass quickly. With the two man rota, our 8 a.m. news bulletin has been suspended, which means a later start at 6.30 a.m. in the news room to prepare the 11.15 a.m. bulletin. Today I shopped and bought 3 tuna steaks (frozen from Seycom) and a couple of tins of my favourite Hungarian Goulash - still only 11 rupees a tin and good value when all other imported food is very expensive. Cocoa and lentils are cheap though.

Health-wise I'm really well - thank the Lord. The only two insect-bite blisters are clearing up and my legs are quite brown so I'm not embarrassed to wear shorts. A colleague has supplied me with a really old fashioned looking radio but it has 5 SW (shortwave) bands and picks up most major foreign stations, including quite a clear signal from the BBC World Service in London. The Falklands is big news here and it only got edged out of today's headlines because of a major Indian political story and the attack on the Pope. We've also reported on Billy Graham's visit to Moscow. I'm getting used, all over again, to the lovely fruit and the cockroaches!

Friday 20th August 1982

*Darling I love you and I hope you weren't too concerned about the events that overtook us during the past few days. It was pretty dramatic stuff really! During the height of the coup we were sitting on the Colen's balcony watching the action through binoculars in and around Victoria and the Airport below. We could see the exchanges of mortar and rocket fire. Army trucks (and ambulances) raced between the lines held by rebel and loyal troops. It was quite tense with machine gun fire on and off for two days in the hills behind us. The radio station was held by the mutineers so we only heard their side, with pleas from the hostages for the government to give in to their demands. For the folks at the transmitter site it was more traumatic because rebels held and shot up the transmitter building and prowled around their houses. I talked to one friend as he was lying under the bed (by phone I mean) while their house was surrounded by gun-toting troops firing wildly at anything that moved.*

*Amazingly as soon as the curfew was lifted at noon yesterday we were given permission to go back on air the next day (today) and I've just finished writing and broadcasting two news bulletins. It's probably drawn us a lot closer at FEBA and we had a super time of prayer and praise on Wednesday night. Because of the coup our mail was cut off and I haven't heard from you (except for the slip enclosed in the Christian Herald) for a couple of weeks. It was good to note that Al has a good car and I hope he's settled in well at Oxford and the vision problem isn't too much of a handicap. How's Chris - do give her a big hug for me.*

*Here are some extracts from an article in the December 1982 CWR (Crusade for World Revival) Prayer Chain Ministry newsletter, Praying for World Revival, titled, An outpouring of God's love.*

*The Seychellois people are very open-hearted and warm, yet their happy way of life has been disturbed in the past thirteen months, first by a coup attempt by mercenaries who flew in from South Africa and then, in August this year, by a rebellion in the army. The loss of life in these events has had a devastating effect on such a small population. The tightening of security and evidence all-around of a military presence has brought tension in place of tranquillity. In the midst of this, however, has come a beautiful visitation from God.*

*John Fear was there when it happened. He was serving his second five-month spell as a news editor for Far East Broadcasting Association, the Christian radio station which transmits from Mahe (the main island on which the capital, Victoria, stands) in twenty-two languages to South Asia, East Africa and the Middle East. He was so thrilled by events that, on his return to England, he talked about them to Crusade for World Revival.*

*When he arrived, John found that there was a great spiritual hunger among the missionaries, "a feeling of discontent with where they'd got to in their Christian experience and with a lack of freedom in worship". FEBA itself was facing a very critical financial situation and the burden of this was not only felt by those responsible for raising money in the home office at Weybridge, but by the missionaries 6,000 miles away and they began to ask, "Why is the Lord testing our faith in making the financial situation so critical?". The missionaries were suddenly faced with a number of quite serious illnesses, mental as well as physical, "that profoundly* affected us as a body of believers," said John. "We felt that as one suffers we all suffer."

With all this happening, the missionaries decided they ought to have a time of prayer and fasting, so they organised a two-day retreat in a quiet house to seek the Lord. One of the striking features of the retreat was the way God spoke through prophecy to a number of people in different ways about putting relationships right. As the Holy Spirit began to move in the gathering, strong-minded missionaries in leadership positions, "quite uncharacteristically, started to confess that they had hidden envies and jealousies towards other families and other missionaries." The more the retreat went on, the more the Lord was breaking through and revealing Himself through changed lives and attitudes.

"There was a very serious sense of wanting to carry the finances," John told me. "Maybe over the 10 years of FEBA's history there's been a sense of them and us - a fairly critical attitude towards the major decisions made 6,000 miles away - a sense among the missionaries that they hadn't been consulted. This critical attitude had to be put right. So we had a love offering - just voluntary, an envelope being left. We wanted to help carry the burden, show our fellowship with the home office and to demonstrate repentance of past critical attitudes towards decisions that had been made." When the envelope was opened at the end of the retreat there was over £900. After that FEBA's financial situation took a drastic turn for the better!

At the same time as God was renewing the missionaries, He was also moving on the Seychellois and non-Christian expatriates. A FEBA family with a burden for the local people had arranged for an evangelistic film to be shown in various places. As John explained,

*"It was the most unlikely means of God reaching people - a twenty-five year old straight preaching film of Billy Graham; no dramatic feature, just Billy face to face. I would have considered it culturally quite unacceptable for evangelism."* John remembers hearing it in the missionary compound, hearing Billy shouting the Gospel and wondering, *"How is it going to be received?"*

*The amazing thing was that in the five quite different environments it was shown in - including a large public gathering in the Anglican cathedral in Victoria and a home group for expatriates who had good jobs - people repented and turned to Christ. John was invited to speak at the expatriates' meeting. During the film, as Billy's uncompromising message rang out, John kept on thinking, "How are they going to accept this?" But there was a move of the Holy Spirit that when John got up to speak at the close he just invited people to give their hearts to Christ and then prayed with them. "Some afterwards said that, though they had come quite critically to the meeting and were almost hostile to the Gospel, they had joined in that prayer. There was evidence in the days which followed that they had given their hearts to Christ."*

*John, who went out to the Seychelles as a stand-in before a long-term missionary could take up the position, is FEBA's first UK-based missionary, available to go anywhere in the world on short-term assignments in critical situations. His latest spell in the Newsroom at Mahe was hectic because of handling such events as the Falklands war, the Iran-Iraq conflict, the Lebanon crisis (such quality news bulletins attract non-Christians to tune into FEBA and encourages them to listen to Gospel broadcasts as well). That was an experience in itself, but it was far exceeded by the experience of witnessing the beautiful way God moved by His Spirit on missionaries and local people alike.*

# Extracts from John's Diary

*The Seychelles are ninety-odd islands in the middle of the Indian Ocean. The archipelago lies equidistantly a thousand miles between India and Africa. Seychelles presents the visitor with a beguilingly beautiful tapestry of endless ocean, palm-fringed beaches and soaring granite hills, all rich in fish, tropical fruit and flora. It has very little history and basically no indigenous population. The 70,000 Seychellois are mainly descendants of French planters and their imported African workers, who now live harmoniously with British colonial settlers.*

*One of the pleasures in life is to relax, in a T-shirt and shorts, by a rickety beach cafe on the beautiful Seychelles shoreline. I can happily unwind there sipping a chilled Seybrew and reading the latest copies of the Weekend Guardian and Times Magazine.*

*In the cool dawn, barefoot girls in neat gingham dresses stride purposefully to school; market traders, wearing grubby T-shirts and baseball caps, set up their stalls with a selection of the previous night's catch of fish or a colourful display of tropical fruit, spices and unlabelled bottles containing unlicensed liquor. The women beat their clothes clean alongside the stream.*

*Wherever I have been overseas I have discovered ways of communicating with Mary - perhaps it could be called Bible-wise. This economical means of communicating meant finding a Bible verse that conveyed in code language my message. A telegram to Mary would read, "Arriving Gatwick 8.30 Saturday. 2 John v. 12, Love John." Looking up the reference Mary read, "Though I have much to write to you, I would rather not use paper and ink, but I hope to come to see you and talk with you face to face, so that our joy may be complete."*

*Typical of the tropics, the period between sunset and darkness lasts only a few minutes. This is the time when mosquitoes do their worst and extract their fill of human blood. Early evening is the most pleasant time of the day. It is still and warm while the air is heavy with the fragrance of many fruits and flowers. A cloudless star filled sky covers the coral protected waters of the Indian Ocean, lapping gently on the shore. It is easy to meditate on the nearness of God in such an idyllic part of His creation. Not even the raucous cries of the fruit bats and the incessant chorus of barking dogs can spoil the inner sense that God's presence is here.*

*Seychelles is publicised as a tourist's paradise. Pity then the poor tourist, given to expect unending tropical heat, who arrives during either of the two main monsoon seasons. Steamy rain beats down unremittingly and when the rain relents the sun bursts through with a scorching heat. The humidity moulds books, mildews clothes and by evening every smooth surface carries a damp film. One spends the night in a dew of sweat so that by morning the bedsheets are wringing wet. Because of its delicate receiving and transmitting equipment the Newsroom provides the duty editor with an air conditioned oasis in which to compile the news bulletins.*

# Chapter 37 - Indian Experiences

John's next foreign assignment was for four months in India. Here one of his duties was to meet with local Christians and take church services as a representative of FEBA. He found Christian leaders in need of encouragement and hoped that he left them feeling their work was appreciated and important.

His contacts with local Christians gave him the opportunity to conduct a large number of interviews for broadcast whilst his presence in India, during some momentous events, meant that he also took on the role of local correspondent.

He also got to meet ordinary Indians and once told us how, when he needed a haircut, he found an itinerant barber squatting on his haunches. The man was so delighted with this unusual customer that he wanted to waive his fees. John made sure that the man was properly paid and got a haircut he was proud of.

## Delhi, 23rd October 1984

*Much has happened since I arrived at midnight on Saturday. I was met and taken to the MGH (Methodist Guest House) - quite primitive dormitory type accommodation with a bucket of hot water for wash and shave.*

*I was collected by scooter to preach at 8.30 am Hindi then English Service at 10 am and 6 pm. Returning at 11 pm I was set upon by a Sikh rickshaw driver who robbed me of R25 - not much but it left me badly shaken. This apparently was a rare occurrence but he was drunk, I think. Everyone here at FEBA has been most caring and I have got over it now.*

Later today I move to the YWCA (yes they take men) in the centre of New Delhi - this will be more comfortable and only £6 a night, incl. breakfast. The MGH is rather isolated near the famous Red Fort in Old Delhi. Tomorrow I speak at a big rally - FEBA's 20th Anniversary - 500 invited guests are expected plus FEBA's Director from Bangalore. So far no sign of tummy upset - eating and drinking carefully.

## New Delhi, 1st November 1984

Greetings from a turbulent India. Although there's not an official curfew, to allow people to attend Mrs. Gandhi's laying-in-state, it's dangerous to go out because gangs are roaming the streets burning down Sikh homes, shops and taxis. There is no action by the police, or fire brigade, but the police and army are massed around here because we are next to a Sikh Temple. According to news reports on AIR (All India Radio) most of the Sikhs in Delhi have fled for refuge into Police Stations and Temples and the army are heavily armed to defend the buildings. Isn't it ironic that the scooter-rickshaw driver who attacked me that Sunday night is probably in fear of his life? I wonder if the Name of Jesus which I mentioned to him made any impact.

All the residents in the YWCA are huddled round the TV set in the lobby which is continuously showing the laying-in state, with the grief bordering on hysteria. AIR play sitar and violin 'mourning' music between news summaries. Late yesterday I had a telex from the Seychelles asking me to phone through a report for their evening bulletin. The voice quality was too poor for broadcasting, but they read the script from 'FEBA's Delhi correspondent' in the studio. I expect they would like a similar report on Saturday's Funeral, Mrs.

*Thatcher arrives for it tomorrow. So I am getting some work I wasn't expecting!*

*The FEBA staff here, fifteen in all, are tremendous people and I have been on the back of four of their scooters. Delhi must have the most chaotic traffic in the world! Cows, rickshaws, ancient buses and lorries jostle for places on the pot-holed roads. Being confined to the YWCA today, I have been enjoying the colourful variety of birds, chipmunks etc. on the back lawns. I think I am now feeling quite at home in India - though Delhi is probably not all that typical. Every walk out is an adventure. Apart from the ever present beggars, cripples and children there is so much to contend with. Take shoe-shine boys - one held onto my shoes for 30 minutes while he tried to sell me everything from drugs to currency exchange (both illegal here).*

## Telegram Message, 5th November 1984

*Post delayed through curfew and funeral but everything fine. Leave Delhi for Bangalore Saturday. Love John v 13-15 (Amp)\*. John.*

\*I had much to write... I hope to see you soon and we will talk together. Goodbye. Peace be to you. The friends here send greetings. Remember me to the friends there.

## New Delhi, 7th November 1984

(Written to Mrs. Margaret Grant at FEBA).

*As you can imagine these have been memorable days in India. Even in the relative calm of New Delhi we were kept under a 24-hour curfew to protect us from the fury of an armed mob who made several attempts to storm the Sikh Temple next door to the hostel where I am staying. There was continuous firing from inside the Temple and two, a policeman and a soldier, were killed as a result of trying to keep both sides apart. The same mob also set fire to and destroyed Sikh-owned shelters and scooters in the road outside. Most of the FEBA staff however live in the suburbs and housing settlements around Delhi and they have seen horrific things during the height of the rioting.*

*It has variously been described as genocide, a holocaust and a massacre. None of them are too strong descriptions for what has actually happened. Our studio technician saw armed gangs mercilessly beat, stab and burn alive over a hundred Sikh men in his district. Even the women and children had fingers chopped off. The local police either stood by and offered no protection or in some cases incited the mobs to violence. Anil, and other staff members, said the worst things were the smell of charred bodies heaped in the street and the sight of the victims' houses being ransacked, looted and burned. Now that the army has moved in, a degree of normality is returning but rumours about communal violence in Delhi or Punjab causes the tension to flare into another bout of violence.*

*Perhaps someone who had the worst experience is a Doctor from the Leprosy Mission. She was travelling from West Bengal by train to Delhi on the day following the assassination. The train was frequently stopped by mobs, with the connivance of railway police and officials. Sikh passengers were dragged off the train and killed, despite protests from the other passengers. The sound of beatings and stabbings was nightmarish. She personally gave refuge in her top sleeping bunk to two young Sikhs, but she doesn't know their fate on reaching Delhi since the boast was that all Sikh travellers into the capital had been killed.*

*FEBA's Urdu programme producer has been visiting the injured in hospitals and refugees in Police Stations and temporary camps, to offer help and comfort in the Name of Christ. Mostly in the latter he found only destitute and shattered women and children whose menfolk had either been killed or fled for safety to woods or fields. The men in hospital were angry because of the humiliation of being forced to cut off their hair and beards. One told him, "The mobs were so frenzied and they told us: you have killed our Mata (Mrs. Gandhi) and we will not spare you."*

*Here at the YWCA we ran out of food and drink. There was to be no bread, milk, eggs or meat in Delhi for several days, except at a nearby luxury hotel where I blew R80 on a meal and shared the dining room with some England cricketers and foreign journalists/photographers here for the funeral. The bar was dry so they weren't in the best of humours!*

*One of my favourite NT passages is the catalogue of Paul's sufferings in 2 Cor. 11 v. 24-33. So for a little foolishness of my own and with apologies to St. Paul, here is my catalogue:*

*Attacked and robbed once - by a Sikh scooter rickshaw driver; what was that message on THE PEACE OF GOD?*

*Propositioned and harassed by assorted drug-pushers, currency changers, a masseuse (I think) and many beggars.*

*Gave eight messages to FEBA staff and received their love and confidence in return.*

*Preached four times in churches, three translated in Hindi.*

*Gave Address at FEBA's 20th Anniversary Rally.*

*Produced four WTB (What They Believe) programmes.*

*Recorded 16 interviews for WTB (six more got away through the curfew!).*

*Queued and filed forms for hours at Airlines, Post Offices, Customs etc.*

*Almost bankrupted by the Indian Airlines rule that foreign nationals pay for internal flights in their own currency (i.e. return ticket Delhi-Bangalore £160).*

*Rode many kilometres on the back of four separate scooters/motor-bikes - one of the drivers was quite mad, especially in Delhi's suicidal traffic.*

*Actually, I am quite enjoying myself and every meal or journey is an uncharted adventure. I am so grateful for the prayers of those who have asked for God's prosperity on the trip. So far I have only suffered one minor cold. Everyone seems to have one because it is the beginning of India's winter.*

*Even though only a visitor to India, I feel part of the all-pervading sadness over the death of Mrs. Gandhi. I tried to convey something of the shock of the assassination in my telephoned report for that evening's news bulletin from the Seychelles. Even hours after her death had been announced, hundreds of thousands of stunned mourners besieged the hospital where her body was being embalmed ready for the laying in state. No one knows what the future holds. Rajiv Gandhi is so politically inexperienced and the tense situation in Punjab could erupt into a backlash of communal violence at any moment.*

Bangalore, 22nd November 1984

*My loving greetings from southern India where I am beginning to thoroughly enjoy life. I feel really well. The early effects of the* mugging, a cold and lots of mosquito bites have worn off and just everything, food, travel and meeting people for interviews is a pleasure.

I am staying in a basic but comfortable flat (rather reminiscent of FEBA's Seychelles flat). Simple cooking of toast, eggs, coffee and tea is possible. Otherwise I eat in restaurants (quite cheap Chinese or Indian dishes). Waiters, however, hover here as nowhere else in the world!

On Monday I went on a four hour train trip to Vellare (in Tamil Nadu) to visit Christians at the Christian Medical College and Hospital there. I spent two nights in Vellore and visited typical mud-hutted villages with the doctors. Obviously I was the object of intense curiosity but it was fascinating.

In theory I should return to Delhi in about ten days' time, but there is so much potential here that I feel tempted to extend the visit and take in a few days in Pune (near Bombay). That could mean I may not be home for Christmas, especially as I have been invited to Calcutta and Mousourrie (in the north of India). I know you will understand that I want to make the maximum of opportunities.

## Bangalore, 8th December 1984

I have been here a month and it has been a continuous flurry of activity. There have been so many meetings, interviews and invitations to meals that I haven't managed yet to visit the main tourist sites.

Have accepted an invitation to stay over in Bangalore to attend and speak at FEBA's carol service in St. Mark's Cathedral on the 14th and a Board Meeting on the 15th so I expect to leave for Delhi during the following week. The possible en route visit to Pune is off because the additional stop-over fare was £50. I think Sez. would like me to report on the elections on the 24th and possibly the 29th. In between times I might get to Jaipur (where the Rhajistan Bible Institute offers good interviewing prospects) and further north to Mousourie.

Health-wise I am fine. A minor stomach upset yesterday but it's gone today. Mosquitoes are a nuisance, even to the locals. I sleep under a net, which is rather too much like lying in a coffin for my liking.

What a tragic place India is! They say the Bhopal killer gas death toll may go up to 5,000. 10 members of the family of one of our FEBA staff (Billy Graham) live within one kilometre of the chemical plant and he can't get any news of them. Over 250,000 people were affected and needed medical treatment.

I am sorry that what few letters I have written have taken so long to arrive. The adhesive on stamps is poor and may have come off one you mention. As you will have gathered everything points to staying beyond Christmas. I will miss you very much but pray you will enjoy a good time together. In any event I will need to return by 20th January as my visa expires then. I don't relish the prospect of arriving in the depths of winter (its winter here and people wrap up in shawls in the evenings but days are hot sunshine as in the height of a good English summer) so I will probably hibernate in Dawn Cottage for at least a month.

There's a continuous cry of vendors going by outside, selling every conceivable thing from bananas and peanuts to a mobile ironing service. I have been puzzled at night, around midnight, by an eerie sound - the loud banging of a stick followed by a long, low whistle. This goes all round the blocks of houses and you can hear it *approaching and then slowly receding in the distance. I thought it had occult connections but when I peeped out last night you can imagine my relief when it was nothing more sinister than a solitary policeman on a bike. He was banging the ground every few yards with his lathi-stick and blowing a whistle. I must enquire but I assume he is advertising his presence to would be robbers (they're called dacoits or miscreants in these parts). The other continuous sound is the whistle of trains, en route to Madras, warning pedestrians and cows on the track. Cows and buffalo-carts are everywhere, plus a few monkeys.*

*I went to a wedding on Wednesday which was very colourful with the bride and groom festooned in garlands. The service was in an AOG (Assemblies of God) church and the message was based on Adam and Eve. The speaker said, "that too was an arranged marriage and like this one it was love at first sight". The reception that followed was totally chaotic and went on for hours with hundreds turning up for food. The bride and groom sat up on a flower-decked platform under an illuminated arch, receiving guests and their presents which were piled all around them. It was the night of one of many Hindu festivals, so fire-crackers were being let off all over the place.*

*Church services take a bit of getting used to. The doors and windows are open so the preacher competes with all the surrounding noises, mainly traffic, dogs and children playing. Men and women sit apart generally and the hymns in vernacular go on and on for what seems like twenty verses each. The pastors are very lowly paid, not as much as a labourer, at least in the Pentecostal/Baptist type churches. People drift in at least thirty minutes after the advertised start and everything is in constant movement, including the ever whirring fans. The praying is very dramatic and fervent but the sermon content repetitive, containing simple Gospel messages. There are exceptions such as Zac Poonen's Bible Studies, to which I went on Monday evening. This consisted of seventy minutes on the last chapter of Zacheriah.*

*I could write a book about India. Chapters would include:*

*THE UBIQUITOUS BEGGAR*

*LIFE ON TWO WHEELS - memorable scooter rides*

*CHANGING TRAVELLER'S CHEQUES - a lesson in patience*

*THE RUPEE - IT'S SPENDING POWER (2 Rupees, i.e. 15 pence will buy: one banana, one box of matches, one daily paper, a glass of iced water and an 8 kilometre ride on a local bus).*

*But that must wait for another day.*

### Bangalore, 16th December 1984

*I have been wondering if I post a letter to you tomorrow whether it will reach you before Christmas or the New Year. Anyway here's hoping and with it comes a special prayer that the Lord will make up for my being away here in India.*

*I reluctantly leave Bangalore for Delhi on Thursday (22nd), reluctantly because it's been a tremendous experience to be among such appreciative friends. I can't count how many homes I have been in, either for house-groups or meals. To sit in a room, smaller than our breakfast room, with 40 people of all ages sitting on the floor leaves an unforgettable memory. One, a Telegu-speaking group, was in a slum area of the city. The total offering amounted to R3 (about 20 pence) and after the message all 40 queued up, kneeling, for a personal prayer of blessing. It was there that I interviewed a former auto rickshaw-driver, now an evangelist.*

*Today I have been with a Tamil-speaking youth group (about 200) and they asked me to speak on 'looking into Jesus' - Hebrews 12. A veteran lady missionary was present and she said the message answered many of their doubts and difficulties. Incidentally, she said she never missed 'First Day' when on furlough and then was surprised to hear we read the news from the Seychelles.*

*Christmas is in full swing. FEBA held its carol service on Friday and a X-mas party for staff, children and friends on Saturday in the office grounds. The children recited and sang, received individually named gifts, carried lighted candles and the adults enjoyed a mutton curry meal. Unfortunately the available water was filtered, but not boiled, so I had nothing to counter the hot curry.*

*I like this flat because I can sleep in on two or three mornings a week and charge my depleted batteries. As far as I can judge, without scales, I haven't lost too much weight, although I probably only have one full meal a day. That's no different to home, though from 9 am to 4 pm the climate is hot and dry.*

*It will be lovely to see the newly decorated hall and the newly licensed TV but do some relaxing now that the latter is legal!*

*Al's scout knife has been invaluable. It has opened sardine tins and lots of locally brewed lager (about 50 pence for a litre bottle).*

Extracts from John's Diary.

*I had been determined to visit the Taj Mahal and on a couple of free days I took the day's rail journey from Delhi. It made an incredible impression on me. It was the most stunning building I had ever seen. Visitors battle through a barrage of souvenir sellers to gaze at the marble memorial that glows with its own sort of light.*

Pavements were stained with blood red splashes of betel juice. Either your stomach can endure it or it can't. Fortunately I survived with regular cups of boiled milky tea, laced with generous helpings of sugar.

Fantastic buffet meals in a 5-star Delhi hotel. Fish, red snapper fillet and carved meat, salad, candied fruit with coffee, braised goat and quart bottles of chilled beer. Meat carved by waiters wearing a chef's hat and white gloves.

Leaving our tourist bus in Agra we fought our way through a barrage of people offering rickshaws, souvenirs and money exchange - all at the usual maximum Indian volume. One insistent man daubed a red spot on my head before I had time to protest.

Slow, white oxen still drag mowers across parks.

I did not quite know what to do when as a guest speaker the church official hung a garland around my neck. Or what to do when men greeted me at such places as railway stations and brushed vermilion spots on my forehead.

During my stay in Delhi I learned to travel, at speed, on the back of a motor scooter. We passed the Red Fort and on through the swarming, crowded streets of old Delhi, before heading along the tree-lined boulevards and vast ceremonial avenues of New Delhi that swept up to the Indian parliament buildings.

Went to India to challenge certain broadcasters and warn them not to use such Pentecostal phenomena as glossalia (speaking in tongues) and healing, particularly if these are made central and indispensable facets of Christian experience. These men understood healing to be an integral part of the historic Christian gospel. The results of healing provide powerful demonstrations of what God is

251

willing to do through the faith of his servants. See the example of the people in Mark 2:3 who had faith in Jesus as they carried a poor paralytic and laid him down in Jesus's presence. He performed the miracle of healing, not in response to any faith the man could have exercised in his condition, but acted on 'seeing their faith', the faith of his four bearers.

During the riots the city was racked by shooting, arson and widespread murder. From my hostel room in New Delhi I could see that the entire night sky was illuminated by flames reaching hundreds of feet into the air. The shanty towns were burning and there was the constant sound of explosions. There were virtually no taxis or auto-scooters as some had come under fire. Some auto-rickshaw drivers were, however, willing to take the risk for a price. Transit through the city under martial law was indescribable. The technique of the driver I was able to hire was to drive down the middle of the road, hooting continuously all the way from outside the Red Fort to the drive leading to my hostel.

Sikhs throng the main railway station in an attempt to escape the city on the few trains still running. The Hindu extremists singled out their homes, shops and cars by mobs in a systematic vendetta against the rival community. Whilst the mortuaries and hospitals were overflowing all the shops, schools, banks and the stock exchange remained closed. When the authorities declared a State of Emergency, troops took over from the Hindu dominated police. They managed to quell the plague of looting and arson whilst extinguishing the religious fury and communal hatred that had engulfed the city.

# Chapter 38 - Return to Seychelles

(Based mostly on extracts from John's letters to Mary)

### Seychelles, 7th March 1985

*I just wanted you to know by this week's post that I am feeling much happier about life in the Seychelles. I suppose I am learning not to be too exclusive in my friendships here because everyone, especially the newer families, want to lavish care and hospitality on me. The weather is very hot but I've absorbed sufficient sun to wear shorts and T-shirts.*

*The present Newsroom rota allows 3 off-duty days in 8 so it's not too bad but I get involved in writing 'Pause for Thought' (six so far) and 'What They Believe' (four produced here so far). WTB is well liked by folk here and when they can't listen off-air (the same programme is broadcast on Sunday lunchtimes and Thursday evenings) quite a few borrow the cassette.*

*I am just watching a gecko crawling along the windowsill and gobbling up ants. Cockroaches still abound, but I have been only attacked by one of the flying variety. There are not so many flowers about as later in the year but the birds are lovely and my one day on the beach so far was very enjoyable.*

### Seychelles, 21st March 1985

*Darling. It's your birthday and since waking this morning I've thought of you a lot. Sorry not to have sent a card and I hope the flowers - if they arrived in time - made some amends. I am also thinking of phoning you if I can get through by direct dialling, but you'll know by the time you receive this letter.*

One of the problems in settling back out here has been to think back to what a dreary person I was during the six weeks between India and Sez. It just came over me in waves of regret. I knew you understood it was because I wasn't well but I just feel I could have made life a little more enjoyable for all of us.

Some of the little things you'll remember about here - a nice big bunch of those small, sweet bananas were on my doorstep this morning. Firing at the nearby range is going on as I talk. There are a fair number of Korean soldiers and I've heard some Cubans are helping to strengthen the security forces here. Anil and I will soon be off to see a video news bulletin at the American Cultural Centre in town. FEBA pay the petrol for that. I now have my own car, a fairly new Mazda, but it doesn't like the hills coming back from Victoria.

### Seychelles, 18th April 1985

I would really love to have your company tonight. Even if we didn't say a word it would be sufficient just to have you nearby. I shouldn't feel low because I've just had a day out on Round Island. What's missing is your own special constancy, which I've probably taken for granted. If so, I'm sorry. As to the details of the day - we went on a glass-bottomed boat and explored the Reef much as you would have remembered it. You can walk around Round Island in about 5 minutes so I did that while the rest went snorkelling. The lunch was probably better than the one we had at Serf Island: Tuna Steaks, Curry Chicken, Salad, followed by a gorgeous fruit salad. After lunch I waded with the kids in the warmest sea I can remember, while the parents slept off their lunch.

One of the highlights of the past week was to meet and interview the New Zealand Prime Minister, David Lange (pronounced Longee). He was on a stopover in Sez. after touring six African nations. As I *am the first FEBA person to have a conversation with President Rene since Douglas Malton handed over the first £90,000 annual License Fee, I thought it would provide a safeguard against any possible repercussions if I recorded the substance of what passed between us.*

*I thought you might find it interesting.*

*Notes of a conversation with Prime Minister, David Lange, of New Zealand and President Albert Rene of Seychelles. It took place after a Press Conference for Mr. Lange at the VIP Lounge of Seychelles International Airport on Sunday, 14th April, 1985 at about 7.15 a.m.*

*(Prime Minister Lange (L) and President Rene (R) were talking together when Lange acknowledged me - I stepped forward and we shook hands).*

*L. I was interested in your question about 'expediency' versus 'principle' in political decision-making. Where do you come from?*

*F. My home is in the South of England - in a beautiful Surrey village called South Nutfield.*

*L. What are you doing in the Seychelles?*

*F. I work for FEBA Radio, as a journalist and broadcaster. We're a Christian radio station and I think we've been operating in Seychelles for the last 15 years or so.*

*L. Is that the same as Radio RHEMA, because I've had contacts with them back home in Christchurch?*

*F. No, it's quite different but I have a friend who works for Radio RHEMA in Christchurch.*

*L. Will you be sending them a recording of this morning's Press Conference? I thought this visit to the Seychelles would be a holiday, but the questions from you guys were quite tough.*

*R. (jokingly and pointing to L) He's been saying that I'm a dictator of a Marxist state but you see we allow a Christian radio station to operate from our territory.*

*F. (laughter) If so, it's a very benevolent one and we're most grateful to be here.*

*L. (jokingly) But you only allow them to operate their station here because it pays your salary.*

*R. (laughing) No, it's because our socialism is broad and tolerant.*

*F. We're very happy to be here. Thank you, Sir.*

*L. (turning to me) Where did you get that quote?*

*F. It was in Newsweek a couple of weeks back (an interview with Lange).*

*L. I think some-one's waving because we've got a plane to catch.*

*F. (laughter) I expect it will wait for you. Thank you, Prime Minister and God bless you.*

*John L Fear ... 15 April '85*

*I still haven't got a car which is a bit annoying after all the promises. It just means that I restrict trips to absolute necessities and I feel justified in asking to borrow one of the other cars. I start teaching the 7-11's Sunday School this weekend (Adventurers). The SS Supervisor has given me a set of Notes and Leaflets for the kids. She told me to do my own thing if I didn't want to use the Course but as the first week is on my favourite NT story (The Road to Emmaus) I can't resist making a play, with 3 scenes, out of it. The expectations of the kids, or at least some of them, according to parents is quite high that 'Uncle John will be our best SS teacher ever'. Pray I won't let them down.*

Seychelles, Boxing Day 1985

(Written to Chris)

*Greetings from a wet and windy Seychelles. It is normally boiling hot, but the Monsoon season has brought the sort of weather wealthy tourists to this paradise island definitely don't expect. I know what you mean when you say that Christmas seems strange in a tropical climate - I had a dip in the Indian Ocean on Christmas Day! How's that for one-upmanship?*

*I am recovering today from a time of unashamed feasting. On Christmas Eve we had two barbecues. At lunchtime a Creole dish of fish with local fresh fruit to follow. In the evening all the 'singles' (I'm an honorary 'single' here not, you'll note, an honourable 'single') and enjoyed barbecued pork on a balcony overlooking the Ocean. Then on Christmas Day I joined a Yorkshire family for their Turkey dinner, followed by Christmas pudding and custard. The evening meal on Christmas Day was the most lavish of all, with Indian, Sri Lankan and American families combining to put on a roast duck, lamb and salad, accompanied by unlimited quantities of Italian Chianti wine.*

*Of course, I am really here to work in the Newsroom. We broadcast a fifteen-minute bulletin to South Asia at 7 p.m. (3 p.m. GMT) and an International Bulletin to South Asia, the Middle East, East Africa and the Gulf States at 8 p.m. It's on several of the SW frequencies and hopefully provides a reliable, up to date and objective news bulletin for the thirty or so countries around the*

Indian Ocean (including India) who are otherwise dependent on news from their government stations, with all that that means.

In addition the three news editors take it in turn to write the Analysis, World this Week and Outlook current affairs features. That's when we turn into instant political pundits. Our Chief News Editor has been a lecturer in political science at Delhi University and a senior journalist with the United Nations in New York so he's well qualified to keep up our professional journalistic standards. We're in competition here with the BBC World Service and to a lesser extent VOA (Voice of America).

## Seychelles, 15th October 1986

It seems as though almost every other day some good thing arrives from you. Yes, the birthday package is here sitting on my desk at home and I must leave it five more days before opening it. Thanks for all the care you've taken to send those things for my birthday. Alastair's amusing letter was almost entirely devoted to how they had tried to dispose of their gift to me because of its alleged unsuitability - we'll see. It was also very thoughtful of you to send The Listener, Private Eye, Beano and above all The Independent. We'd heard quite a bit about the launch of the new daily so it was especially good to see a copy, which I thought was very good.

Thanks for the various news items about family members. I am pleased that Chris has got over the initial down and that Al & Judith are moving into their own house at last. Did you have a good time with Robert? Thanks, Mary, for your prayers over the Pentecostal Church. I felt the first Sunday was the best. We started at 11 a.m. and by the time the Communion Service was finished it was 1.45 p.m. The second Sunday I dipped into other people's ministry. A bit *of David Pawson here and a bit of David Watson there and I don't think the Lord was able to use it as much as if I had stuck to things I had discovered to share first hand. Incidentally, the fact that my interpreter fainted half way through the sermon didn't help either. He's quite a young chap in his 30's but I think the heat got to him. He finished off, once he'd come round, sitting.*

*A busy, but not untypical, day in the life of John Fear in Seychelles*

*(14th November 1986)*

*8.00 a.m.   Woke to the sound of running water and found the bathroom and hallway flooded due to a broken fitting in the toilet.*

*8.30 a.m.   Prepared for breakfast and discovered the remains of instant coffee solidified, owing to an ill-fitting lid, and had to be content with less stimulating Milo instead.*

*8.45 a.m.   My Bible Reading (and I really am enjoying The Living Bible, given to us at the Evangelist's Conference in Amsterdam) included the promise, "They who wait upon the Lord shall renew their strength". I needed that promise!*

*9.00 a.m.   Found local estate manager and he promised to fit a new toilet part on Monday. Fortunately there are alternative facilities in my house.*

*9.30 a.m.   Arrived in the Newsroom and sorted some of the overnight copy from Reuters news agency and monitored the recorded early morning news bulletins from France, Israel, Australia, India, Washington and, of course, the BBC from London.*

*10.15 a.m. Made a start on scripting Analysis (our Friday evening current affairs feature) having decided to do a piece examining the student rebellion in South Korea, in which radical* students are trying to force reunification of their half of the peninsular with the communist North.

*10.25 a.m.* The first party of eight journalism students, together with their two tutors, from the local Polytechnic arrived for a visit to the Newsroom.

*10.40 a.m.* The second batch of nine students arrived (both had earlier sat in on a live broadcast of the hour long Mosaic magazine-style programme to the Middle East). Both groups said they enjoyed that experience and their look around the Newsroom so their appreciation made up for the mug of FEBA coffee I missed because of their visit.

*10.55 a.m.* Jan Hanekom (South Africa) and I gave the Polytechnic group a sort of seminar on writing and broadcasting an international News Bulletin. It was well received and I was invited by their senior tutor (a former Chief News Editor at Radio Seychelles) to give a lecture at the Polytechnic on interviewing.

*11.45 a.m.* Arrived home for lunch and while the ham thawed out from the freezer (what would I do without a fridge-freezer?) I finished off the piece on Korea and scanned a newly arrived news magazine from India.

*1.30 p.m.* Met my new 'house girl' and just had time to show her the floodwaters, clothes, washing-up, etc., before heading back up the hill for the Newsroom (with FEBA's help I have bought a really old 'banger' mini estate car but I'm thankful for it because I would never make it up there in the midday heat - in the 90's).

*1.40 p.m.* Discovered that David Huntley who normally reads Analysis is unable to do so because of a prior engagement and so I persuade an equally busy Derek Knell to record it instead. He said it was interesting - thank God for a Barnabus!

2.00 p.m.    Began writing the 7 p.m. Bulletin for South Asia. It was a good day for News with major regional stories coming in from India, Bangladesh, Sri Lanka and Afghanistan. Finished it in time for Christopher Singh to broadcast his Hindi translation of the Bulletin at 6 p.m.

3.15 p.m.    During the tea-break I had a good conversation with a local staff member about a personal problem. It's rewarding to see friendships growing between missionary and Seychellois personnel.

5.45 p.m.    Returned home to find a spick and span house, with no signs of floodwater and a beautiful added touch, a large jam jar full of tropical flowers from my garden.

6.15 p.m.    Back in the Newsroom to update the SA Bulletin and write the headlines. Also on my desk is an Air Seychelles flight ticket with a provisional booking to return home on 16th February.

6.50 p.m.    Prepare the Control Room self-op combo desk ready for tonight's transmission of the News and Analysis (which is ready on a remote controlled tape recorder in an adjoining studio).

7.00 p.m.    Read the eleven minute Bulletin live and mercifully free of a cough that makes reading such a strain (this has been my fifteenth live read in eight days).

7.11 p.m.    Analysis follows without a hitch.

7.20 p.m.    A major story from Reuters clatters out on the teleprinter. It is a report on an international U.N. anti-pollution conference in Geneva. This needs to be completely rewritten and a couple of earlier items on the Philippines and Iran need to be updated for the 8 p.m. World News Bulletin. Rewrite the headlines and introduce new ones.

7.59 p.m.    Back in the control room. Unfortunately the operator gives me the 'red light' over a minute early (i.e. before prayer and a drink of water) so in consequence I had to hit the 'cough switch' a couple of times, but would any listener be as aware of the pauses as I am? I doubt it!

8.15 p.m.    Clear up the Newsroom and prepare for overnight Reuters copy and cassette recordings of tomorrow morning's overseas Bulletins.

9.00 p.m.    Wrote the script for Christian News Report (a weekly 5 minute programme on Christian activity, around the world, but with an emphasis on what's happening in our target areas) ready for recording tomorrow and for broadcasting on Sunday at lunchtime in India. Thanks to Keith Bowers, who telephoned a good piece from London, on TEAR Fund's emergency aid grant to the flood victims in the north Indian state of Assam, it will have particular interest for our listeners in India.

10.15 p.m.   I wrote this journal for the day and thanked the Lord for someone out there who had been praying that I should experience this day the truth of the promise that, "those who wait upon the Lord shall renew their strength".

11.15 p.m.   Dressed ready for bed and then sat to meditate on my balcony, where a brightly lit cruise liner and a Soviet battle cruiser dominate the ocean below. Listen to a ministry cassette, a Bible Reading from 1 Peter by Donald English at the Keswick Convention, (Donald's is surely one of the loveliest voices in the British pulpit) and, praise the Lord, spotted a cockroach swimming around in my fresh lime juice before drinking it!

Seychelles, 9th December 1986

*I'm a bit pushed for time this week, so I thought you wouldn't mind getting my news, especially about the Pope's visit, from a letter I wrote to an Indian friend this week, Rayla Rajpillay.*

*"Dear Rayla,*

*I really appreciate receiving your letters. This is the third and I think we are quite 'kindred spirits', apart from sharing many of the same interests. It was good to work and have fellowship with you in Amsterdam and when I hear your programmes here I praise God for the flair He has given you as a communicator of God's truth.*

*Since we said good-bye in Holland I had a few short weeks at home but it was the best time of the year with the harvesting of fruit and vegetables from our garden. It doesn't get any easier for Mary and I to part, this time for six months, but there is 'sweet sorrow' in parting and it's far easier to bear than the desolate pain of rejection, which I've also experienced here.*

*A highlight for us this week was the visit to Seychelles of Pope John Paul. As a journalist I got the opportunity to go to the Airport to meet him off the plane from Australia and then I recorded his sermon in the Sports Stadium here. The big question for us was how acceptable it would be to South African Protestant Christians if we broadcast too much of what he said and did. In the event I included a two-minute report in the 7 p.m. and 8 p.m. Bulletins and a fuller five-minute report for our Christian News Report programme on Sunday lunchtime. We were all fascinated to know how this 66 year old veteran was so fresh after a 50,000 kilometre tour of six countries when aides and journalists with him on the plane were hollow-eyed and pale. I asked an aide about this and he said,* "perhaps it's because His Holiness spends those long flights reading the Psalms and the Prayer Book" (what a challenge to us)."

I've been feeling so much for you anticipating the upheaval of going to Uganda. To be honest I am feeling less and less certain about it, so don't feel that it's anything more than a possibility (rather than a probability) at this stage. When I hear how much people here and in India appreciate 'What They Believe', I wonder whether I wouldn't be better concentrating on keeping that series going, with further visits to India, Pakistan, and Sri Lanka.

My desk is in a mess and just for the moment I have mislaid your letter, so I'll try to respond to any points in it next time I write. As you probably gather from all the typing errors, I am pretty tired but I thought it would be a good idea for a change to catch the Wednesday flight post and see how quickly that reaches you.

P.S. Tell Judith she's a clever girl and look after the babe. I suppose one shouldn't ignore Al - so I will. Love to them both please.

# Chapter 39 - African Challenge

John's next assignment was to help train radio broadcasters and enable them to produce effective health and farming programmes for broadcast to East Africa. He was seconded to a previous employer, TWR (Trans World Radio).

## Nairobi, 29th July 1987

*Although I've only been here a week it seems to have been more like a month, things have been so hectic. TWR folk have given me the warmest possible welcome and it seems exactly the right moment to have come here.*

*After a few days in a hotel I am now installed in a nice modern flat. It is cleaned daily and although I need to cook there are shops nearby. I have my own car, a Datsun, so can work late if necessary without fear of mugging after dark.*

*Just now I'm listening to commentaries from the All Africa Games here in Nairobi. This is on the very efficient Sanyo stereo radio cassette recorder I bought at Heathrow for £97. Expensive but it picks up BBC, FEBA & TWR beautifully!*

*TWR has taken a 3 month lease on the flat, so it looks as though I will be here until at least the end of October. There's still plenty to be done.*

*The flight out was good but tiring. I was met at 6.15 a.m. Although it's mid-winter the African sun is quite hot and I haven't seen any rain yet.*

Nairobi, 12th August 1987

*We have been given a day off by President Moi. I'm not sure whether it's because it's the closing day of the All Africa Games or because Kenya are playing the soccer final against Egypt, probably the latter because it wasn't a scheduled holiday! Anyway Nairobi is in carnival mood with flags and banners everywhere. It's quite chilly for Africa though with the rains coming about a month early.*

*Let me tell you about this flat. It's rather posh actually and most of my neighbours seem to be diplomats. The four storey flats are built on the three sides of a large grass quadrangle. As I am on the ground floor the kids are a bit noisy during the day. A balcony leads off the large sitting room/dining area. The kitchen is well equipped and there's a nice bedroom and bathroom.*

*Apart from hard work during this week - which is really appreciated by everyone - I seem to be getting involved in quite a bit of travel. Last Sunday I preached at an Anglican church in Nakuru which is halfway to the Ugandan border. It's about 200 kilometres from Nairobi and the road passes through the spectacular Rift Valley and Masai tribelands. Next Sunday I go to Meru which is a third of the way to Ethiopia. There I am to speak at the Induction Service for an Africa Inland Church pastor. The TWR General Secretary takes me on these journeys (he seems to like showing me off!) in his rather nice Datsun car. Then, next month I am expecting to go to Lusaka in Zambia for a week's Council of Church's Conference.*

*During the first two weeks in the office I seem to have covered a lot of ground, including taking a dozen workshops on interviewing, script writing and voice presentation. To help me with the latter I have recruited an elocution teacher from the Kenyan Institute of*

Mass Communication. In addition I have been out and about with trainee interviewers and feature writers. Most of these have come from a newspaper background so they need to adapt from the written to the spoken word. I have also chaired a sub-committee to hammer out a policy on music to be used in the Africa Challenge programme. As it's secular music there are quite divergent views but there's been a good spirit of give and take.

I'm just listening to the football commentary on the radio (Malawi vs. Cameroon) and he's just said, "The clouds are looking heavy but we know God is with us so it won't rain. But if it does rain we'll accept it as one of God's blessings."

### Nairobi, 6th September 1987

I guess it's quite a while since I wrote but that doesn't mean I haven't thought about you. It's just that life is pretty hectic and when the weekends come I just flop out to recover. Actually, today (Sunday) has been quite a heady mixture. I went to the national stadium for a football game this afternoon (that was very entertaining) and to the Anglican Cathedral (All Saints) for their Evening Service. A deaconess gave the sermon on the Beatitudes and it was excellent.

I am not sure whether to go to Zambia next weekend or not and I won't be able to decide until a colleague returns from his two weeks holiday on Wednesday. There's still so much to be done here as well. The weather is quite hot during the day now and I've had a few mosquito bites at night, so there has been a change. A couple more staff members have had me for a meal. It's apparently unusual for Western visitors to get these invitations so at least I know I am not intimidating. It occurred to me as I watched football this afternoon that I feel somewhat disorientated culturally these days. It probably

267

comes from spending extended periods in different cultures. I begin to get absorbed into them, then move on and take a bit of each with me. It's the first time I've had this strange feeling of not knowing quite where I belong.

Thanks also for your earlier letter giving me the domestic news. FEBA are very good as they send me their Prayer Notes every week and that also keeps me in touch. Africa Challenge starts on FEBA Radio tomorrow and it's also on VOK (Voice of Kenya) on Saturday evenings. Other African national radio stations are also expressing an interest in having it, so that's quite rewarding for the team. Africa Challenge sounds good now we've stepped up our ratio of interview features. I had better close as I still have my weekly discussion paper to write for tomorrow's planning meeting.

### Nairobi, 26th September 1987

Please forgive the long silence from this end. I thought of writing often in the past week or so but never actually got down to it for various reasons.

Your welcome letter, with all the family news, arrived and I hope you had a really enjoyable family weekend together. Things here are going reasonably well, I think. The main reason I didn't go to Zambia was because of the critical stage we had reached in training and stepping up productivity. I really feel now that everything would have slowed down if I had taken that week away. It was a disappointment, not only to me but to my colleague who rather likes showing me off and getting me speaking opportunities!

The so called 'long rains' have just begun and should continue through October and November. I am told these will make the red, dusty roads more pleasant to travel on and turn the arid desert *areas green. You have a Kenyan map I think, so I'll mention that I hope to spend a week at the lakeside town of Kisumu. This will be partly a much needed break but also an opportunity to interview two or three key people involved in development work in that needy part of the country. I also have an invitation to preach again at that large Anglican Church, half way to Kisumu, at Nakuru, so I'll try to fit that in too.*

Nairobi, 17th October 1987

(Written to Al and Judith)

*A wave of sadness swept over me the other day when a letter from Mother said that Alexander was six months old on the 3rd and is now sitting up. I am really sorry to miss these growing up days and only hope that what I am doing here makes up for it in the end. To be honest I am learning as much as the team I am trying to train. They are learning about the radio techniques of script writing, presentation and interviewing and I am being introduced by them to all the mysteries of their African culture. For instance, there are strong arguments for retaining some of the traditional tribal customs we in the West have always written off as uncivilised. Just in the last week we have produced programmes dealing with female circumcision, burial customs, polygamy, extended families (versus nuclear families) and dowry/bride price. To see these issues through the eyes of indigenous African Christian leaders is a real education. Their faith and practice is firmly based on the teaching in the Bible but they regard the wholesale condemnation of these customs by Western missionaries as having undermined the positively cohesive influence and stability of the tribal system.*

*Our programmes are aimed at helping the rural peoples of Africa. On Monday the theme is child care (six preventable diseases are*

269

massive killers because of ignorance about inoculation) and on Tuesday we deal with growing food crops that provide nutrition for individual families. So one week it could be poultry, bees for honey, goats for milk or meat and another on maize and other vegetables. We work closely with the WHO (World Health Organisation), UNESCO (United Nations Educational, Scientific and Cultural Organisation) and University teachers here in Nairobi. They pour out written and recorded materials that we try to disseminate so that it's of practical help to illiterate and poor people in villages.

Another interesting aspect to the work is that we sometimes clash head on with governmental no-go areas. This especially applies to AIDS in East Africa; Family Planning in West Africa and racial and human rights in Southern Africa. The programmes are heard throughout continental Africa as they are broadcast both from Swaziland and from Seychelles. Voice of Kenya also broadcasts selected editions of the 30 minute programme as does Zambia Broadcasting Company, so at times we are walking quite a tightrope. Once we are satisfied with the format of our English language programmes and audience research analysis we'll begin broadcasting in the main African vernacular languages with the same material.

I was encouraged the other day when reading in Matthew's gospel the response of Jesus when the disciples of John the Baptist questioned his authority in caring for the physical and social needs our Lord encountered. He said, "Tell John how those who were blind can see. The lame are walking without a limp. The lepers are completely healed. The deaf can hear again. And the poor are hearing the Good News". So, hopefully, for His sake we bring cups of clean water, nutritious recipes, health care and the courage to struggle for freedom.

Honestly, I didn't intend going into such detail when I sat at this typewriter (a Brother deluxe 660TR) but as you may gather I am quite enthusiastic about this unusual and difficult assignment. Incidentally, the BBC World Service have devoted a major part of their Bulletin to the storm damage (they describe it as the worst since records were kept) in southern areas of England. Sounds quite horrific.

I was very pleased to receive your joint letter of 25th September and thanks, Judith, for the birthday greetings at the end - I think this is my third consecutive birthday overseas, i.e. India, Seychelles and now Africa. Glad you had an enjoyable weekend at Dawn Cottage and I look forward to filling that empty chair at Christmas.

As there's a lot of blank paper to go let me tell you about my likes and dislikes of Kenya:

I like the cheapness of local products. You get 30 Kenyan Shillings (Ksh.) to the Pound Sterling. In markets the most beautiful tomatoes cost Ksh.5 a kilo; fish (especially Nile perch fillets) cost around Ksh.10, enough for two meals; potatoes are Ksh.4 a kilo and I'm also getting to like local chilli sauce which costs Ksh.7 a bottle compared with Ksh.30 for imported tomato sauce or Ksh.40 for Coleman's Mustard. Beef, lamb, pork, chicken, goat and buffalo are all very inexpensive, although the last two are invariably tough by our standards.

I also like the weather. At the Nairobi altitude of 8,000 feet it's sunny and cool with a profusion of flowering shrubs everywhere. I like the variety of things to do: nearby game reserves, the national museum, Masai villages just down the road along with shops and restaurants in Nairobi. The British cultural centre put on a free film show every Tuesday evening at 5.30. Last week it was David

271

*Putnam's Local Hero. It is a haven for expatriates and we all enjoyed the quirky British humour in that film. I also enjoy the overflowing churches and the lively African worship with lots of dancing to drums! TWR folk are friendly and I get invited to their homes for meals occasionally. A couple of our most hospitable staff are Asian so I get an Indian meal, though they've never left Africa.*

*Among my dislikes are the mad drivers, dodging in and out of the potholes at reckless speeds. Most vehicles pour out clouds of thick black smoke. The noisy African neighbours and servants in this block of flats. Everyone seems to shout and no-one has learnt the art of quietly shutting a door. The way men manhandle women and children out of the way in their attempt to get into overcrowded buses. The Louts!*

*As the rains are overdue, red dust is everywhere. Only the main roads are covered in tarmac, so everyone seems to have a perpetual cold from the dust and traffic fumes. I am fed up with local radio stations. Kenya, Tanzania and Uganda dominate the airwaves and they are all equally nationalistic. VOK invariably begins every news bulletin with what 'His Excellency Daniel arap Moi' said and did during the last twenty-four hours. I've never heard a comedy show, drama, concert or anything remotely creative. The diet consists of music, mostly western pop; news, with thinly veiled criticisms of a certain neighbouring country; worthy but immensely dull development programmes and quite a bit of religion of the preaching variety.*

*So that's the blank space taken care of. The likes come out on top and as its Saturday afternoon I'll probably do one of my other likes, which is to take the old Datsun out, without a map, and head in an untried direction out of Nairobi and see where it takes me. As this letter partly explains why I missed out on Alexander's early infancy you may wish to store it away among his newspaper/magazine archives so that he can judge in due time whether it's an adequate excuse.*

*NB. This letter copied to Mother and Chris so they know how things are here.*

*Also Rob, so that's the entire dynasty!*


On the way home, in November 1987, John stayed overnight at an airport hotel in Nairobi and became poorly with a virus. Back in England he went into hospital in Redhill. It took a long time for him to recover from that unknown virus.

# PART 8 - RETIREMENT

John and Mary

# Chapter 40 - Retirement Years

The following three chapters were written and compiled by Alastair Fear.

John and Mary sent out a regular prayer letter to associates and friends. In the December 1990 edition, John's retirement from FEBA was announced:

*"At times this year we've been tested, almost to the point of despair, but with Paul we gladly testify, "We have this treasure in jars of clay to show that this all surpassing power is from God and not from us."*

*A few weeks ago my doctor signed me off from work, for three months, as my heart and lungs were no longer able to cope with the strain of travelling and preaching. However, this has meant that I have been able to spend more time in my study. It's been a lovely time of rest, reflection and research but also a time when clouds of doubt have threatened to stifle my prayers."*

Those three months soon became a permanent retirement and John's study became his bedroom as the journey upstairs became too difficult. He enjoyed visits from all the family, especially his grandchildren. There was a game he loved to play with Joseph, who would come to him and chatter away. John would listen very carefully and when the tale finished he said, "RUBBISH!" As this was a regular game they both roared with laughter.

There was a large collection of books around the walls of his study. Many had been collected over twenty years before when John had visited second hand bookshops in search of biographies, letters and sermons from Spurgeon, Whitfield, Moody and many other notable Christians. On one wall there was a large tableau of photographs. This had begun with a dozen black and white photographs of colleagues, from the Billy Graham days, arranged neatly beneath the glass. Gradually other photographs, of people he wished to keep in mind during his prayers, were slipped in around the edges. Charismatic Arthur Blessett, lumping his cross around the country, rubbed shoulders with Mother Theresa, whilst a group of FEBA children and parents from the Seychelles shared a corner with Cliff Richard.

At the time John wrote the following:

*"During the year immediately following my retirement, I had time to reflect deeply on how much I had failed to live by my Christian principles and on what an imperfect witness I had been to the Grace of God. There were incidents I regretted and times when I said things that were unkind. All of these needed time to bring to God and seek his forgiveness. Wherever possible I wrote to those whom I had wronged. At the same time I was grateful for all the opportunities I had been given for serving the Lord."*

John swapped his study full of old books and the large house, which had been the family home for 23 years, for a modern bungalow in Cumnor, a small village on the outskirts of Oxford. This move bought John physically closer to most of his family and also gave him the chance to discover the English countryside. During the summer and autumn months of 1991, John enjoyed exploring his new surroundings: the Cotswold villages, the ancient buildings of Oxford and the River Thames. He described these outings with great enthusiasm.

Cumnor is closer to various cross-country routes than South Nutfield was. Many friends called to see John. Some visited him on a regular basis, coming from Sevenoaks, Worthing and Bristol.

Because of his illness he did not feel able to form new relationships and so these long-time friends were his Christian fellowship and support.

There was more time for John to enjoy the company of his grandchildren. On one occasion, whilst Mary was away, John invited them over, along with the children of an ex-TWR colleague. Crepe paper, baubles and paper chains were provided and the children had a great time making the rooms look festive for Christmas. Once a few of the more bizarre touches were removed, such as baubles cellotaped to door handles, it was ready as a surprise for Mary.

At this time John wrote to his favourite Uncle Bob, with whom there had been no contact since Exclusive Brethren days. Uncle Bob responded with letters that John read aloud to other family members. John also began writing to and phoning his brother Paul and sister Mary, with whom he had not communicated for years. Paul and John planned to visit old haunts when their respective healths were better. Then came the reconciliation with Robert, his eldest son. John had started writing a book of his life but progress was arduous and slow until Robert became involved and offered to type up the notes onto his computer.

In the new year of 1992, John went as an outpatient for a series of tests at the John Radcliffe Hospital in Oxford. His heart had reverted to much the same state as when he had needed the operation twenty years before. Unfortunately they uncovered other problems that would need treating before a heart operation could become remotely possible.

A new dressing gown and pyjamas were purchased to initiate this new phase in John's retirement. Things had changed since the seventies when he had his heart operation. Hospital wards were now mixed and John was surprised to see lady patients wandering about in dressing gowns. The doctors explained how they would put a tube down John's throat through which minute microscopes and cutting tools could be inserted and manipulated.

Despite the wonders of modern technology, things were not easy for John. It took him a long time to recover from the endoscopy operation that removed gall stones. For him it was like major surgery because his reserves were so low. On one visit, I remember him having great difficulty working out the position of a Test Match between England and New Zealand. John felt he was fighting against becoming institutionalised. Drugs were beginning to affect his state of consciousness. He was dependent on a cocktail of medication to keep his body functioning, to ease the pain and help him sleep.

He relied on Mary's constant visits. Two other stalwart visitors were the Pastor of the Grace Baptist Mission and the Catholic Priest from the local parish. Both, in their different ways, helped John as he tried to turn his eyes to Jesus and not be dragged down by despair.

On one occasion he was wheel-chaired down to the Hospital Chapel where someone was reading aloud from a book containing other patient's requests for prayers. John kept asking the reader to carry on. It was as though learning the fears and hopes of fellow patients helped give a new perspective on his own situation and brought him some peace.

John experienced night fears, dark presences that visited him during the hours of darkness. After arriving home, there was no respite from these fears and he began to hallucinate quite vividly. On one occasion he telephoned the police, after midnight, because of the presence of an unknown person in his bedroom. This was a worrying time for all who visited John. Then the Doctor decided to change John's painkillers. The hallucinations and delusions vanished but the pain became more raw and less tolerable.

Confined to the few rooms of the bungalow, John spent many of his waking hours listening to the radio. He gleaned small snippets of information from the local BBC Radio Oxford and wrote notes such as, 'For Alastair - Louden Wainright will be performing in Oxford next week' or, 'For Mary - an elderly lady is opening her garden to the public for the first time this afternoon. Entrance fee 50p. Times and places are all provided'. We were all supplied with cuttings from newspapers and nuggets of information.

Nothing was too parochial. He wrote to the local village magazine (Cumnor Parish News) when it appeared in a stunning new format:

*".... your predecessor was imperfect in the style of its presentation but therein lay much of the charm. Many villages are losing their traditional magazines as desk-top computers have replaced the trusty duplicator in village halls and vicarages. It was always a red letter day when the old CPN popped through our letter box. I will miss the delightful tones and the authentic voice of our rural community, both of which were found within its pages."*

The next crisis came in the early summer of 1992. John was losing a lot of blood and had to go back to the John Radcliffe with a near fatal bleeding stomach ulcer. There followed an operation and a week in intensive care where the dark pressures and hallucinations crowded round him again.

On one occasion he asked a young physiotherapist to pray with him. The young man delivered an embarrassed and faltering rendition of the Lord's Prayer, something that had not passed his lips since school days.

Soon after returning from intensive care to a normal ward, this dark other world began to disappear. There remained another slow physical and mental battle to recover to a better state of health. I remember at that time he would listen and question other Christians closely as he sought to get to know more about his Lord. It was not a subject on which he had all the answers anymore. With the priest, the pastor and other friends, there were important differences in interpretation that John needed to rethink.

The bungalow was prepared for John's return with the help of an occupational therapist. Hand rails appeared by doors and a fold down seat was put in the shower. At home Mary succeeded in getting John to eat again, providing him with small and simple meals such as scrambled eggs and creamy soups. In hospital, food had not agreed with him and cartons of high protein drink accumulated, unopened, by his bedside.

John and Mary worked on more reminiscences for the book. Slips of paper went into brown envelopes for the sections on Billy Graham or the Seychelles. He had enjoyed writing up his childhood and early marriage, recalling events that had not been remembered for years, but some of the intervening years had been more difficult to write about. He wanted to be straight and truthful but did not want to hurt others or accentuate differences.

# Chapter 41 - Looking Back

During the years, John had been called on many occasions to occupy the pulpit in both small and large churches. He would usually find an anecdote from personal experience to help illustrate his sermons. These were not pre-planned. John hoped that God would bring them to mind at the most appropriate time, during the course of a sermon, to illustrate some spiritual truth.

When John was too poorly to write, Robert (who compiled and edited these memoirs) turned the tape-recorder on him one evening and got John talking. It was an important evening for Rob as it had been many years since the two of them had been alone together, happily talking for hours on end. The result is one such anecdote that has been transcribed from that evening's tape.

The personal experience John related was intended to help younger Christians who were struggling, without much apparent success, to testify to the effect on their lives of being a Christian. John's message would be that God sometimes hides from us those things which He is undoubtedly achieving through us (perhaps by speaking a word to a school friend or colleague, distributing tracts or even preaching in the open air), since the evidences of success could easily spoil the simplicity of our message. John's anecdote is reproduced below;

*"I was invited to preach in a church for the first time when I was aged about 20 and I was, of course, enormously flattered to be given this privilege and responsibility. I think that, when we are young, we devote ourselves to tasks such as this with great enthusiasm. I was no exception. I found an obscure verse in the prophecy of Hosea, in the Old Testament, on which to present the*

message of this first sermon. I should mention that I was given six months from the time of the invitation to the date when the sermon was to be delivered. During this lengthy period I prepared, very conscientiously, to deliver the best sermon I was capable of. Having selected the verse, I studied the commentaries available to me to be sure that I got the context of the text right, the meaning of its teaching right and the application that I could make to the ancient text relating to practical Christianity in the 1940's.

In the course of preparation I did such practical things as rehearse the delivery of the sermon in the front of my parents' dressing room mirror, getting the hand movements correct and timing the duration of the sermon so it fitted into the forty minutes which had been allotted to me. In short I couldn't have been better prepared for any particular task to which God had called me before or since.

At last, the morning arrived when I was to deliver that first sermon. When I opened the curtains I discovered that the heavens had opened and a cloudburst was descending on Leicester, where I lived, and I needed to cycle 40 miles to the city of Newark on Trent where I was to deliver the sermon. Incidentally, I was wearing one of those heavy surplus army greatcoats that you could buy from the Army & Navy stores. It was already heavy enough but by the time I had cycled about a mile, from my home on the way to Newark, it had taken in enough rain to have the effect of doubling my normal weight.

It was a pretty boring ride because the road from Leicester to Newark, for those of you who know it, is a long straight road of 40 miles between two hedges. However, I was quite undeterred because I was buoyed up by the expectation of being able to preach a long prepared sermon to a church full of eager people.

*At last I arrived in Newark and you'll never know the disappointment I felt when I stepped behind the small pulpit desk to be confronted, not by a church full of people but, by a congregation of exactly three; two middle-aged parents and sitting between them a teenage boy.*

*I can honestly describe them as being typically phlegmatic English people who looked on this phenomenon of a youth, virtually standing in his own baptistery with the rain which he had bought into the church, preaching his heart out from an obscure verse in the prophet Hosea. I had intended to preach for forty minutes as this had been the time the many rehearsals had lasted. However, I seemed to lose my poise and stormed through the whole sermon in less than ten minutes.*

*Can you imagine how I felt during the 40 mile cycle ride back from Leicester? To put it mildly, I had a running argument with God about what he was playing at, giving a young fellow a task for which I assumed He would provide a responsive congregation who would appreciate the months of preparation that had been put into that sermon. Every turn of the pedal I persisted with this complaining. I constantly complained to God that He had let me down and that was the last thing that I was ever going to do for Him. I heard nothing about the occasion again.*

*Twenty years later it was arranged for me to go to Newark on Trent, to speak at a preparation meeting for the Billy Graham television relays that were being held in Leicester in 1966. (As you will have read I was fully engaged in the preparation for becoming a member of the committee.) I went to Newark to speak at this preparation meeting and I spoke about the need for all Christians, young and old, to commit themselves to preparing, as best they could, in prayer, financial giving and getting the local press and population familiar with the programme of meetings which were to be held in Leicester.*

*In short, this was a very different type of meeting to the one I had spoken about with such sparse results twenty years previously. In fact, I felt it would be appropriate to quote the previous occasion of apparent failure, in order to challenge the young people to take on the preparation without worrying too much about whether they were apparently successful or not. I told them of my failure on the previous occasion and said that I was sure that if God had called us to do something for Him, He would crown it with success. I was getting old enough now to appreciate that this was the principle upon which He worked.*

*As I stepped down from the pulpit and walked down the aisle, through the crammed congregation, a young fellow stepped into the central aisle, grabbed me by the shoulder and asked, "Do you remember me?" I said, "No." He was very excited and disclosed that he was the young man who was a member of that congregation of three, twenty years previously. He said that he was so challenged and impressed by the fact that the young fellow would give up his Sunday to come and tell him about the love of God and how he could know forgiveness of sins he, there and then, committed his life to God and had since entered the full time Christian ministry."*

# Chapter 42 - Final Days

On Christmas Day 1992 John was well enough to visit us in Abingdon for the afternoon and a meal. He had devised a number of family games, one of which involved some blindfold masks and a bag full of variously shaped objects. Alexander and Jessica enjoyed trying to guess by touch what the objects were inside the bag. We were forced by the children to play that game again and again on succeeding visits. John had a good way with the children but these bubbling encounters left him exhausted for the rest of the day. On later visits we only allowed the children a quick peep in to see Grandpa.

In 1993 a bad chest and difficult cough had begun to take over his life. The only way he could cope with the cough was to sit on the side of his bed. We could not get him to lie back comfortably on his pillows as this would aggravate the cough too much. John began to live in a twilight world with the radio on, listening to Radio Oxford & Radio 4 during the day and the World Service during the night. He would sometimes doze off and be found flopped forwards with his head on his knees. This went on for what seemed months until his capacity to breath became so limited and the effect of the cough on that limited capacity became life endangering. He returned to the John Radcliffe Hospital for another series of investigations.

Nothing conclusive came out of the tests. They tried bombarding John with antibiotics to try to shift a chronic infection that completely incapacitated one lung. The heart operation and a return to good health were no longer possibilities. We did not want to see him continue to suffer like this.

Mary was planning to visit Lisieux with a Church group for a week. Unfortunately this coincided with John's return home from Hospital. Chris and I arrived at a plan to share the care of John for a week but his health was too precarious and Mary stayed at home.

Before the end of that week John was back in hospital with a total renal failure due to the effect of some drugs. It was during this hospital visit that John got definite news of his condition - he had cancerous cells in his right lung. He seemed lighter in spirit than he had for some time in the weeks following this news. It meant that his painful condition was no longer interminable. There was an end in sight and for Mary it meant that there would be more support, from nurses and a local hospice, in looking after John.

John consciously set about rounding off his affairs on this Earth. With Mary and Rob's help he sketched out the chapters for the book that he might not finish. The latest news was communicated to relatives and friends. Legal and financial affairs were organised. He wrote down how he would like his funeral and memorial service to be conducted. Surprisingly this did not involve a list of hymns and bible passages but a list of people who were to be invited and asked to contribute. He left it to their discretion what should be read and sung. He chose photographs to be included in the book - they were laid out in a large frame at the bottom of his bed. The window sill looked like a florist's shop with many lovely plants and bouquets from friends.

Mary had to be near at hand because John often needed the oxygen and nebuliser by his bed and was not well enough to administer this himself. The slightest exertion, such as being lifted up on the pillows, was followed by a couple of minutes recovering with the oxygen mask against his face and vapour pouring from the nebuliser.

In early October 1993 John went to the Michael Sobel House, a hospice attached to the Churchill Hospital in Oxford. In contrast to the John Radcliffe Hospital, the hospice was a place of cool shade, homely furniture and peace. The food came in small appetising portions, like those served at home, although even these were hardly touched.

John commented about the only man sharing the room, "He is very ill", perhaps not recognising how ill he was himself. It was evident to visitors that the end would not be far away now. He got to know a Christian nurse who prayed with him during the stay. He had a lot of visitors during the week. Most people saw him for the final time here.

The priest had offered to give him the sacrament of healing but on his arrival John preferred a friendly chat instead. The ceremony was rearranged for the following Tuesday when Mary could be present. Having watched the spiritual pilgrimage of Malcom Muggeridge with interest, he had been attracted by the Catholic Church, although not understanding various parts of the teaching. He was, therefore, having talks with the priest during the last weeks of his life.

After returning to the bungalow John spent most of his last two days asleep. Mary had been praying in the adjoining room when she heard him cough. John indicated to her that he needed oxygen. The mask pressed to his face did not bring the necessary relief. He joked, "It doesn't seem to work". Then he dropped the mask and coughed a few more times before relaxing back on the pillows.

Mary soon realised that this was no ordinary sleep. He was probably not aware of what followed; how we joined hands with his hands, still warm, and said a tearful prayer; how we lit a candle and put on some gentle music, as though to waft his spirit away up to God. This was more for our own sakes than his. The things of Earth were probably already growing strangely dim for John. As friends and colleagues commented during his funeral, "If anyone had a place reserved for them, it was John".

Even after John had gone there was the privilege and fun of continuing to spread his love through the legacies left to some friends and colleagues. We were once more aware of the 'twinkle' in his eye as folk had their breath taken away by these unexpected gifts and as they enjoyed getting something personal. Comments received included: '...made speechless', '...quite astonished' and 'people bequeathing money to us is not the sort of thing we're used to'.

# EPILOGUE

Late in 1989 I reached the age of sixty. Until a few years ago I detected little decline in my physical vigour but ten years in the tropics have taken their toll on my physical powers. Although the youthful passions of the flesh are spent, I do not notice any decline at all in my curiosity, amusement or enjoyment in the ordinary blessings of life.

*"Oh God, stay with me, let no word cross my lips that is not Your word, no thought enter my mind that is not Your thought, no deed ever be done or entertained by me that is not Your deed."* (The Daily Prayer of Malcom Muggeridge).

Looking back on life I would like to have been less preoccupied with myself, less dependent on the opinion of others, while remaining undisturbed by their criticism and unaffected by their praise.

God is considerably nicer than we have ever given Him credit for.

When I have been particularly ill I wondered if I would be afraid to die. I now believe that although I am ready to go because the future is assured, it is instinctive to want to live and at the same time to feel nervous about the unknown process of dying. But I draw reassurance from the words of St. Augustine who said, "Entrust the past to God's mercy, the present to His love and the future to His providence."

I have come to the inescapable conclusion, far too late in life, that it is better to be loving than to be right.

I just pray that being in the immediate presence of the Lord will not be an unfamiliar experience; having, I trust, already known Him in a limited way in this life.

John L Fear, Cumnor, Oxford, August 1993.

# APPENDIX

Did you enjoy this book?

Then please leave a review as a tribute to John Fear's exceptional life.

Thank you.


Get in touch with me, Robert Fear, via my Blog, Facebook page or Twitter (links below):

Blog: www.fd81.net

Facebook: www.facebook.com/fredsdiary1981

Twitter: @fredsdiary1981

You can also chat to me, along with other memoir authors and readers at: We Love Memoirs, the friendliest group on Facebook:

www.facebook.com/groups/welovememoirs

If you want a personal introduction to WLM, would like to be added to my mailing list, or simply ask a question, please e-mail me at fd81@assl.co.uk.

You might also be interested in my own memoir Fred's Diary 1981: Travels in Asia

UK: www.amazon.co.uk/dp/B00H1POOKO

US: www.amazon.com/dp/B00H1POOKO

# MORE PHOTOS FROM JOHN'S LIFE

Paul, James, Grandma Harwood, Mary & Elizabeth

Fear Family group including Uncle Bob, Aunty Betty and Uncle Jack

Great Grandfather Charles A. Line, Grandpa Jock, Aunty Beryl and Peter

Holiday group including Grandma Ethel Line,
Olive and Ralph Lynes, Beryl Line and Mary Grace Lynes

Groby Pool: Mary's first Leicester visit with Mary, James and Elizabeth

Paul and Gundola's Wedding: Mary, John, Paul, Gundola and Elizabeth

Robert, Grandma Lynes and Mary

Robert and Alastair

John, Christine and Robert

Alastair, Robert, Christine and Penny

The Fear Family

John in the Seychelles

John with Joseph

Judith, Alastair, Jessica and Alexander

Alexander

Joseph

Jessica

# ACKNOWLEDGEMENTS

John wrote chapters 1 to 26 himself. Chapters 27 to 35 have been built up from his notes. Bill Spencer of Evangelism Today added some information to the Billy Graham era. Chapters 36 to 39 were compiled from John's letters and extracts from his diary. Alastair wrote the final chapters and Robert recorded the manuscript on computer and edited it.

Grateful thanks to all others involved. Honor Ward who supplied information about the Line family. Roger Heath who lent what may be the only interview done with John as an interviewee! To all people seen and unseen who have been part of John's life. Also, to Peter Smuts who produced the book after original consultations with John and then Robert.

For this most recent edition my heartfelt thanks go to:

Ida from Amygdala Design for the fantastic cover

Members of the WLM Beta Readers Group

The supportive team at Rukia Publishing

YOU - for your wonderful review

Printed in Poland
by Amazon Fulfillment
Poland Sp. z o.o., Wrocław